COSMIC CRYSTALS

The hidden world of crystals and the New Age application
of crystal energies.

D1042541

COSMIC CRYSTALS

by

RA BONEWITZ

TURNSTONE PRESS LIMITED
Wellingborough, Northamptonshire

First published 1983
Second Impression May 1984
Third Impression September 1984
Fourth Impression April 1985
Fifth Impression August 1985
Sixth Impression November 1985
Seventh Impression February 1986
Eighth Impression May 1986

British Library Cataloguing in Publication Data

Bonewitz, Ra
    Cosmic crystals
    1. Crystals
    I. Title
    548   QD905.2
    ISBN 0 85500 205 0

Turnstone Press is part of the Thorsons Publishing Group

Printed and Bound in Great Britain by
Whitstable Litho Ltd., Whitstable, Kent

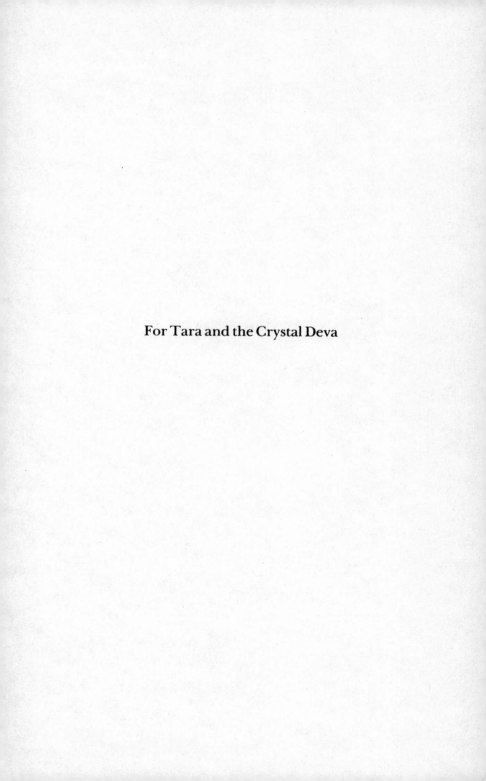

For Tara and the Crystal Deva

Contents

Introduction

For most of the twentieth century, science and religion have dwelt in separate houses, suspiciously peeking through the curtains at one another. But the mystical side of man cannot be long locked away, and many mystical hearts beat in the bodies of pure scientists. The last twenty years, corresponding with the dawning of the Aquarian Age, have seen these mutual suspicions progressively beginning to melt. While we have not yet embraced one another, there are many scientists and mystics who have at least begun to talk things over.

There often seems to be a conflict between science and mysticism, and yet the scientist and the mystic seek the same thing — the Truth. But until recent times, the scientist has sought the truth behind the form, and the mystic has sought the truth behind the essence of form. It is only today, particularly as recent advances in science give us an opportunity to discover that form is just a specialized arrangement of energy (which is what the mystics have been saying for thousands of years), that we at last discover common ground for a marriage between the two.

Although readers of this book will perhaps consider themselves to be more mystically than scientifically inclined, let us not forget that were it not for rational science we would still believe the Earth to be the centre of the universe, and would be as far as ever from realizing our oneness with the Cosmos and the greater universe of Spirit. We must also remember that 'reality' inhabits neither the world of the material nor the world of the Spirit in its entirety but dwells equally in both. Thus, if we seek reality, we must look in both worlds, and when we do, the reality that we discover is the oneness of both.

With my background in the physical sciences I have had an opportunity to dwell totally in the world of the material; and yet as a spiritual awakening took place, I have also had an opportunity to dwell in the world of the Spirit. This has been an unique opportunity to see both worlds, and the relationships between the two. It is this marriage of matter and Spirit that has given birth to this book.

In the following pages we shall discover the physical aspects of crystals, as well as their esoteric properties. Although we study them separately, let us not forget that they exist together in the same space and time, and are totally part of one another.

We live in a world of form as well as spirit — so now let us look at some very precise forms, and how they have come to inhabit the material Universe.

1.

In the Beginning

Children of the Universe — Sons of the Cosmos —
Brothers of Stars. So the race of man is described by some
recent songwriters.

Perhaps this is a strange beginning for a book about the
mineral kingdom, but if we find truth as well as poetry in
these lyrics the questions and implications raised are all
part of the greater question of the relationship between
matter, spirit and man. This is not a book about esoterics,
and yet esoterics cannot be separated from matter and
minerals, as they are one and the same. Writing as both a
scientist and a mystic, I find no conflict between science
and mysticism; nor do I believe it is any accident that the
greatest advances in science are coming at a time when we
are once again beginning to rediscover our spiritual roots.
As we shall soon discover, we are indeed Children Of The
Universe, and Brothers Of Stars. And one thing the
songwriters have thus far missed — Cousins of Crystals.

Let us begin at the beginning by turning the clock back
— back 15 thousand million years, to the beginning of the
universe itself, or at least the universe as we would now
recognize it. Back to the time when all of the matter in the
universe was contained in one unimaginable large ball,
floating in the void. Not matter as we know it now, made
up of atoms and molecules, but a vast ball made up of the
very building blocks of atoms themselves — protons,

neutrons and electrons — a vast 'soup' of potential matter.

How long this seething mass of proto-matter had been in existence, and what it was doing *before* it came into this state, is unknown; but at this point, some 15 thousand million years ago, it began to rapidly expand and fill the void. It not only expanded rapidly: it exploded.

All the matter contained in the hundreds of thousands of stars we can see in the sky at night, and the thousands of billions of stars that we *can't* see, was contained in this vast cosmic firecracker, so one can easily see why scientists refer to this event as a Big Bang.

There are other scientific theories about how the universe formed, the most prominent of which is the Continuous Creation Theory, in which matter is being constantly formed and is likewise constantly disappearing from the universe. This theory was particularly prominent up until about 1960, but with the advance of radio astronomy, and with the information being gathered from space probes, the evidence is continually mounting against these other theories and in favour of the Big Bang.

But this is science. Do we have any evidence for such cosmic events in mythology? It turns out that we do.

From China we discover in the P'an Ku myths:

First there was the great cosmic egg. Inside the egg was chaos, and floating in chaos was P'an Ku, the Undeveloped, the divine Embryo and P'an Ku burst out of the egg, four times larger than any man today, with a hammer and chisel in his hand with which he fashioned the world.

And if we look into the Hindu religion, we find the idea that the Cosmos itself undergoes an infinite series of deaths and rebirths. In the Hindu system, there are a number of time scales, which correspond rather well to our current concept of the universe. Its cycles run from our ordinary day and night, to a day and night of Brahma, which is 8.64 billion years long. This is longer than the age of the Earth or the Sun, and about half the time since the Big Bang.

The Universe, then, is the dream of a god who, after 100 Brahma years, dissolves himself into dreamless sleep; then, after another 100 Brahma years, he awakens and recomposes himself, to once again dream the cosmic dream.

At the beginning of each cosmic cycle, the creation of the universe is represented as the cosmic dance of Shiva in his manifestation as the Dance King. In this manifestation he has four hands: in the upper right hand is a drum whose sound is the sound creation. In the upper left hand is a tongue of flame, a reminder that the newly created universe will, billions of years from now, be utterly destroyed.

These images, both Chinese and Hindu, are thousands of years old, but are they so unlike the conclusions of modern science? In fact, the next discovery for which science reaches is the discovery that the universe will indeed contract at some time in the future, going back into its 'Universal Egg' state. At this very moment, scientists throughout the world are studying the universe in the attempt to discover whether or not there is a certain critical amount of matter in it — an amount of matter that will make the universe pull back together gravitationally, and ultimately draw back inwards on itself. Is there any doubt what the answer will be?

Every religion accepts that the formation of the universe was a deliberate act by some form of Creator, so can we simply not accept that the Big Bang merely represents the physical outworking of the fact of creation? And is this not merely the first step in the continuous Act of Creation that *is* the universe?

But what does this have to do with the mineral kingdom? The mineral kingdom is certainly the oldest kingdom in the universe, and if we can accept the premise that the formation of the universe is a creative act of God, then what we discover in the mineral kingdom must have a great deal to do with what God had in mind as He began the creation of the universe.

Let us turn back then to this first act of creation, the Big Bang, and see how the physical universe has evolved.

In that inconceivable cosmic explosion, the universe began an expansion which continues today. As space stretched, all the matter and energy in the universe expanded with it, and then cooled rapidly. The early universe was filled with radiation and vast amounts of matter, mostly hydrogen — the lightest and simplest element formed from elementary particles in the cosmic fireball. Most of the Universe is still made from hydrogen, but in the beginning there would have been little to see as the atoms would have been distributed uniformly. But then, one by one, the atoms of hydrogen became attracted to one another by their minute gravitational pulls. Gradually, localized pockets of gas began to form, and as they did so the gravitational attraction of each of these little pockets for other particles of gas began to grow also. Vast accumulations of such pockets began to form, great sinuous clouds stretching across the cosmos. Gradually, these localized pockets began to grow denser, as more and more particles of hydrogen were entrapped. Eventually, these immense gaseous clouds began to spin and flatten, to later form the galaxies.

But within these embryonic galaxies, much smaller clouds were also becoming denser through gravitational attraction, and in the centres of these clouds, temperatures and pressures began to rise. Finally a point was reached at which the hydrogen atoms began to stick together, to fuse and form the gas helium.

This fusion, this marriage of hydrogen atoms, has an interesting by product — light. And so the first stars were born to light the skies.

These proto-stars, unlike many of todays stars, had plenty of hydrogen fuel to burn. This type of star evolved rapidly, lived fast, and died young. Yes, died. Stars go through the same birth-life-death cycle in their physical bodies as we do. And it is in the dying of stars that new birth takes place in the universe. This is because of something else taking place in the centres of stars during their life cycle. The fusion process does not end with hydrogen becoming helium. The heliums begin to fuse, forming carbon; carbon fuses to form oxygen, and by adding further heliums, silicon, sulphur, iron and other elements are formed.

In the dying stage of this type of star, then, it first expands to become a Red Giant star. One such star, Alpha-Herculis, now in a near-death stage, is 580 times the diameter of our Sun, and would fill all the space from the Earth to the Sun.

In the final death stage, this type of star explodes in a brilliant supernova, scattering its core of 'stardust', its core of heavy elements, into the universe from which it was born.

Ultimately, one such cloud of thermo-nuclear dust was attracted to a newly-formed, rather ordinary yellow star towards the distant edge of one of the arms of one of the newly formed galaxies. Once again, as with the formation of the stars themselves, localized pockets of this denser matter began to form. The gravitational attraction between these denser particles would have been much greater, and therefore these localized areas would have begun to attract new matter quite rapidly. Eventually, through the process of attracting more and more of these particles (accretion), large balls of dense matter formed, circling this relatively new yellow star — and the Earth and other planets were born. Unknown to most of us, the process of accretion goes on even today with thousands of tons of cosmic matter, usually in the form of micro-meterorites, dumped onto the Earth each year.

As the Earth coalesced from the solar dust cloud, the force of gravity began to draw the heavier elements towards the centre, and eventually pressures became so great that melting took place. This caused a further sinking towards the centre of heavier elements, especially iron and nickle. The central portion of the Earth, called the core, (Figure 1), is still molten and is about 2000 miles

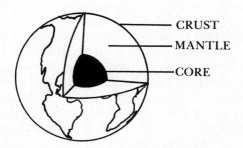

Figure 1   Section of the Earth

in diameter. It is thought that the friction between the rotating Earth and the molten core, which tends to 'slip' inside the Earth, creates much of the energy that causes crustal movements, discussed in later paragraphs.

The Earth is still quite hot inside, and no matter where on the Earth you are located, all you would need to do is go down a few miles, and the temperatures would be hot enough to boil water. Imagine what the temperatures must be like going down *thousands* of miles! Nor does the Earth seem to be cooling off very much. Many of the elements which make up the outer portions of the Earth are undergoing radioactive decay, which in turn releases more heat into the Earth's body.

Moving outwards from the core, and making up almost the remainder of the Earth, is the Mantle. The mantle is composed mainly of very dense, crystalline rocks, iron and magnesium rich. Due to the tremendous heat and pressures involved, much of this rock remains in a 'plastic' state, a scientific term meaning that it is relatively flexible and easily deformed.

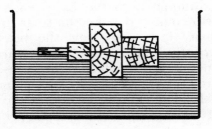

Figure 2   Blocks of wood floating in water

Floating on top of this flexible mantle, made up mainly of lighter minerals, is the Crust. Strangely enough, floating seems the exact word that applies. Studies have shown that the crust is very thin under the ocean basins, but under the continents it begins to thicken, and under the mountain ranges is the thickest of all. Figure 2 shows a number of blocks of wood of different thickness floating in a basin of water. We see that the thicker the block of wood, the more of it extends below the water level. We find exactly the same situation in the crust. Figure 3 shows a typical cross-section of the Earth, with an ocean basin on the left and a continental mass on the right. Studies have shown that the thicker the material on the continent (i.e., mountains), the thicker the material below. We can see from this illustration that the material of the crust behaves exactly as the blocks of wood — the thicker the material, the deeper it extends into the mantle.

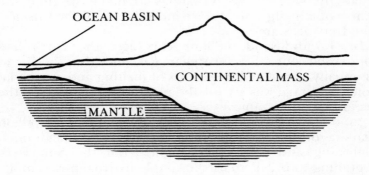

Figure 3   The crust floating on the mantle

This concept of continents floating also helps us to visualize how it is that continents move. The study of continental movement, called Plate Tectonics, has shown that at one time in history most of the continents were all in one mass, and that they subsequently broke apart. The most obvious evidence of this is the close fit between the coastlines of South America, and Africa, and it is thought that the motivating force for these continents to move is the heat generated in the interior of the Earth, as mentioned earlier.

As the deepest holes drilled into the Earth have gone down little more than five miles, much of the information about the inner portions of the Earth is derived from other scientific methods. Information about the core and inner parts of the mantle are mainly derived from the study of earthquake waves and how they are bent as they pass through matter of different densities. Rocks from the upper mantle can often be studied, because many deep-seated volcanoes may bring up material from eight or nine miles deep, often well into the mantle.

In the preceding paragraphs we have followed the evolution of the physical body of the Earth, the evolution from pre-matter through elemental hydrogen, to the dense material at the centre of dying stars. Now, let us be reminded of our own physical bodies, and look into the history of the Earth to see how they came about. As we do so, let us remember that there is not a scrap of matter that makes up our own bodies that has not had its origin in the centre of a dying star. We are indeed Sons of the Cosmos, Children of Stars!

By 4.6 thousand million years ago, the Earth had condensed out of inter-stellar gas and dust and had essentially completed its process of melting and consolidation. The stage was set for the next act of creation — the beginning of organic life.

In the primitive oceans, perhaps around 4.0 billion years ago, the first stirrings of life were beginning. Lightning and ultra violet light from the Sun were beginning to break apart the simple hydrogen-rich molecules in the primitive atmosphere. These molecules were then recombined into more and more complex forms. The products of this early chemistry were dissolving in the oceans, forming a rich, organic 'soup', which provided the building blocks for the more complex life forms that evolved later. The mineral kingdom was also beginning to break down chemically, providing additional 'material' for organic life.

Exactly how these first life forms began to organize themselves is not known, but a recent theory suggests that certain organic molecules began to attach themselves to certain types of clay minerals, and that the crystalline patterns of these clay minerals served as a template from which more complex life forms developed. It must be emphasized that with this theory, it is not the minerals themselves that are evolving as life forms: they merely served as the *patterns* over which organic life forms were built. These life forms were well adapted to the hydrogen atmosphere of the Earth at that time and Creation waited for the next step.

By about 3 billion years ago, the oceans were beginning

to fill with blue-green algae, and it was this evolving algae that set the stage for the next pattern of organic development.

Green plants produce oxygen. By about a billion years ago, the oceans were not only full of algae, but other simple green plants as well. Because all these plants were generating oxygen, for the first time the Earth's atmosphere began to have large amounts of free oxygen in it. Although almost all life is now dependent on oxygen, it was quite poisonous to many of these early life forms, and many of them died out en masse. New plants began to develop that were more compatible with the new atmosphere, and animal life also appeared.

By 500 million years ago, the oceans were teeming with life, and were dominated by large herds of trilobites, which looked rather like large insects (Figure 4). During the latter part of this same time period, called the 'Cambrian' by geologists, the ancestors of modern clams and shellfish began to develop.

Figure 4   A trilobite

Up until this time, life had been limited to the oceans, and it was not until about 440 million years ago that the earliest land plants appeared; at about the same time, in the sea, the fishes were beginning to form.

One day, around 345 million years ago, a fish with particularly strong fins discovered that he could support himself on them, and moved for short distances out of the water and on to the land. It was from this first intrepid explorer that all land-dwelling forms originated. By 200 million years ago the reptiles were beginning to dominate the Earth, particularly the group known as dinosaurs. This domination was to continue for the next hundred and thirty million years, until about seventy million years ago. The dinosaurs died out quite suddenly, possibly because of a cosmic catastrophe — a collision between the Earth and large asteroid, or perhaps a comet. The dust from this event would have raised planetary temperatures to a point intolerable for large reptiles.

It was during this period of domination by the dinosaurs that the continents began to drift in earnest into their present positions.

By the time the dinosaurs died out 70 million years ago, the face of the Earth had changed radically. The Americas had drifted away from Africa and Europe to form the Atlantic Ocean; Australia had drifted away from the mainland, and India had drifted northward to collide with Asia, pushing up the Himalaya mountains.

As the dinosaurs died out, the surface of the Earth was left to animals who were able to regulate their body temperatures, and who were thus less vulnerable to planetary changes — the mammals. Man's earliest ancestors appeared no more than seven million years ago, a mere instant ago, geologically speaking. Our earliest *recognizable* ancestor has been around for a million years at the very most. Only 129 million years to go to catch up with the dinosaurs!

What we are seeing then, is a flow of creation, in which one stage leads to the next, with each new stage becoming more aware than the last.

First, there was the great cosmic explosion, leading to the next stage of creation — the formation of the elements. Then, a period of consolidation, leading to the formation of stars and galaxies. Then, another period when stars began to evolve into heavier elements, followed by the death of those stars and the scattering of those heavy elements back into the universe. Then, another period of consolidation as the heavy elements began to form planets. As for the Earth itself, first there was the evolution of the Earth's body, through melting and recrystallization from the solar dust cloud, and then another long period of consolidation on the surface as the earliest life forms began to appear. This was followed by another evolutionary stage, as the early life forms created the atmosphere, causing in turn another stage in the evolution of plants and animals capable of living in such an oxygen-rich atmosphere. There have been successive stages since then, when one form of life has come to dominate the Earth, only to set the stage for another form to succeed it. Can any of us think that this process ends with the race of man?

Many spiritual sources teach us that we are in a new stage of evolution even now with the coming of this New Age of the Earth, the Aquarian Age; but we are also being taught that this is an evolution in consciousness, and it will be the pattern of evolved consciousness that new life forms will take.

It is significant, then, that at a time when men are becoming much more sensitized to the world around them, the very earliest energies of the universe are the last ones we have become sensitive to. We have tended to think of the energies of minerals as the lowest form of energy, but seen from the standpoint of the evolution of the universe, the mineral kingdom formed under the *highest* energy conditions and therefore, in a sense, represents the *highest* energy to which man can attune. For these energies carry the very imprint of the creation of the universe, and having chosen to live in a world of crystalline matter, we therefore align ourselves with the same creative impulse, the so-called 'Thought in the mind of God', that is the motivation of the universe.

And do we not have this same aspect of creativity that is our very spiritual nature, our own 'divine spark'? Do we not have this same ability to visualize, to see in our mind's eye, some object and then go out and build it? Is this perhaps what we mean when we say that man is made in the Image of God?

Herein lies the key to the very existence of the race of man — that is, we *are* a part of the Divine Essence that *is* creation; we are here on the Earth to participate in that creation.

Man is a synthesis of matter and spirit within himself — a being of spirit encased in a body of matter, which is a perfect microcosm of the universe itself — the Divine

Being whose body is the physical universe. This synthesis is vital to the evolution not only of man but also of the Earth itself.

Why? What is it we are here to do?

Think back for a moment to the beginning of this chapter — the universe is still mostly made of hydrogen, the lightest and simplest element. Look at the sky tonight, and what do you see? Thousands of stars — and beyond them there are thousands and thousands of millions of stars that cannot be seen. Doing one thing. Taking hydrogen and making heavier elements out of it. The universe is getting *denser*. The whole pattern of evolution of the universe itself is from lighter matter to denser matter.

But as the physical universe becomes denser, doesn't the Spirit also need to begin to inhabit that denser matter? And isn't that exactly what we, as beings of Spirit, are learning to do on the Earth?

We have been thinking of ourselves and the Earth as some kind of a spiritual backwater: we see ourselves as being encumbered with these awful dense bodies that we have to drag around, and we look forward to the time when we can slough them off for good.

It has been useful to believe this, but the truth is finally dawning for many: what we are really here to do is exactly the opposite — to regain our enlightenment as a spiritual race, and begin what we were created to do. To learn, not how to escape from matter into spirit, but how to reach up into spirit, and bring spirit down into the denser realm — to infuse matter with spirit.

All we have to do is look at other planets in our own solar system to get a clue about this. The Earth is the only one where this is taking place. We are not at the tag-end of spiritual evolution — we are at its cutting edge!

We began this project of working with the matter of the Earth quite well. From our own level of spiritual awareness we were working with the whole of the Earth, especially with its crystals, through the use of large and powerful crystals — working to enlighten the very matter of the Earth itself. But then, mostly through lack of experience, it began to go wrong, and man began to forget his tie with creation. And Atlantis fell.

At this time of the spiritual renewal of the race of man, called the Aquarian Age, we are just beginning to remember our tie to the physical as well as the spiritual universe, and as we begin to re-learn about crystals, we begin to re-learn about our own synthesis of matter and spirit.

Although in the following chapters on crystals the physical and spiritual aspects are sometimes discussed separately, it should never be forgotten that they are totally part of one another.

2.

The Atom

In the first chapter we looked at the macrocosm — the universe. Now we turn our attention in the opposite direction, to the microcosm — the atom.

It is only within the last few decades, through the development of modern technology, that we have begun to understand the inner workings of the atom. Even so, scientific knowledge of the atom is still incomplete, and although we are beginning to understand *how* it works, we are still woefully lacking in the knowledge of *why* it works. In this chapter, we shall discuss the mechanics of the atom and in particular, the mechanics that relate to how atoms attach themselves to one another. This is necessary in order to understand the inner workings of the crystal and how the crystal relates to energy. Most of the effects we observe in the use of crystals, both esoterically and exoterically, relate to their unique arrangement of atoms. Although the description given herein of the mechanics of the atom is much simplified, it covers the essentials necessary for an understanding of crystal energies.

The atom is made up of three main building blocks — *protons*, *neutrons*, and *electrons* (Figure 5). Protons and neutrons are about the same size and weight and form the central portion of the atom, called the nucleus. The proton has a positive electrical charge; the neutron is electrically neutral. Electrons are very tiny particles with a negative electrical charge, and are much smaller than protons or neutrons. Electrons circle the nucleus at relatively great distances, like to travel in pairs, and arrange themselves in specific layers, called shells, around the nucleus (rather like the different layers of an onion), each shell corresponding to a different level of energy. These shells of electrons fill from the centre outward, with each shell having a maximum of eight electrons that can occupy it.

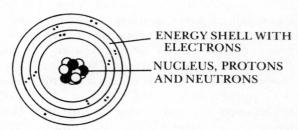

ENERGY SHELL WITH ELECTRONS

NUCLEUS, PROTONS AND NEUTRONS

Figure 5   The atom

Since the atom tries to maintain electrical balance, the positive charges of the nucleus are usually balanced exactly by the negative charges of the electrons. It is also possible to have unpaired electrons in the outermost shells and still maintain the electrical balance. It is these outermost shells that are of the greatest interest to us in our study of the mineral kingdom, as it is the movement of the electrons in the outermost shells that are responsible for many of the effects of energy that we observe in crystals. It is also in these outer electron shells that bonding of one atom to another takes place to form the unit cell, which we will discuss later — the building block of crystalline matter.

It is important to realize that electrons do not move freely from shell to shell: they move only when their energy has been increased or decreased by a specific amount. We call this amount of energy a *quantum*, which is a multiple of the energy of a photon of light. It is perhaps useful to think of each of the electron shells, and the quantum leap from one shell to another, as being like rungs on a ladder. It is not possible to step up half a rung.

Although protons, neutrons and electrons are the basic building blocks of the atom, recent studies have shown that they themselves are further made up of even smaller particles, and that these smaller particles appear to be made of pure energy. So, at last, science is coming to the conclusion that matter is just another form of energy, which is exactly what the mystics have been saying for the past four thousand years at least! Some of these sub-atomic building blocks have rather interesting names, such as *quarks*, *neutrinos*, and *mesons*. These particles are incredibly small, and pass quite easily through 'solid' matter. The Sun is a great emitter of neutrinos, and in the time it takes you to read the word 'neutrino', about a hundred billion of them have passed through your body. It doesn't even matter if you are reading this at night (when the Sun is on the opposite side of the Earth) as the Earth is almost as transparent to neutrinos as is your own body. This raises the question: How solid is 'solid' matter? If the nucleus of an average atom were the size of a tennis ball, the electrons would be smaller than a grain of sand, and the outmost would be circling at a distance of *four miles*. 'Solid' matter is, in fact, mostly empty space. If you were to squeeze all the empty space out of your own body, you and several friends could easily dance on the head of a pin!

Matter may take three forms — solid, liquid and gas. In a gas, the atoms are at some distance from one another and have relatively slight attraction for one another, leaving them free to move about at random. In a liquid, the atoms are much closer together and have an electrical attraction for one another, although not enough to lock them rigidly into place. Certain types of liquids can be cooled to a sufficiently low temperature at which the atoms become quite inactive and tend to have little freedom of movement, although they do not form any sort of definite pattern. When such a super thick liquid exists at room temperature it is called a *glass*.

In a solid, the atoms have considerable attraction for one another and fasten themselves rigidly to one another. Not only are the atoms held rigidly in place, but they also form very distinct and repeatable patterns. Such matter is said to be crystalline. This does not necessarily mean that the matter will form crystals however, and the difference between these two states (crystalline versus crystal) will be discussed in the next chapter.

Bonding

With the exception of a very few liquids that take on crystalline properties under certain conditions, we need only concern ourselves with the solid state of matter in our discussion of crystals. An understanding of the forces that attach atoms to one another within the crystal is most important, as it is disturbances in these attaching energies that are responsible for many of the effects that we observe from crystals in energy fields.

The first type of atomic attachment (called bonding) that we shall examine is called an *ionic bond*. This is nothing more than electronic attraction between ions of opposite charge. An ion is formed when an atom gains or loses one or more electrons, creating electrical imbalance. Loss of an electron by an atom yields a positive ion, while gain of an electron yields a negative ion. Figure 6 shows a crystal structure formed from ions. In this instance, the sodium atom (Na+) has lost one electron, and the chlorine (Cl−) has an extra electron. As atoms of these two elements come in contact, the extra electron of the chlorine atom pops over to the adjacent sodium atom, causing electronic attraction. Likewise, the sodium atom is attracted to the next chlorine atom, and so on.

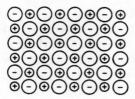

Figure 6   An ionic crystal

Ionic bonding is a particularly strong type of bond, and crystals with such bonds are usually quite tough although, interestingly, they are often quite brittle. These crystals often have very good *cleavage*, which is when the crystal breaks in flat planes. Figure 7 shows why. As we have said, an ionic crystal is made up of a series of alternating positive and negative electrical charges, and, as with the ends of a magnet, when two poles with the same charge are opposite one another, they repel. As is shown in the figure, all we need do is slide the structure of the crystal for the width of a single atom, putting positive opposite positive, and negative opposite negative, and the crystal literally breaks itself apart along the plane of the atoms. Ionic bonding however, is not the most usual type of bonding found in crystals.

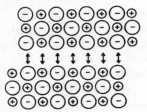

Figure 7   Cleavage in an ionic crystal by repulsion

The most common type of bond is the *covalent bond.* In this type of bonding, the outer shells of the two atoms involved (and they can be atoms of the same element) are not completely filled, although the atom is in electrical balance. Since the energies of the atoms will always try to balance, if such an incompletely filled atom comes in contact with another, then both will try equally hard to fill their outer shells. But in this case, rather than one atom giving away its electrons to the other, as in the ionic bond, these two atoms 'decide' to *share* their outer shell electrons. As mentioned earlier, electrons like to travel in pairs; the other rule that they like to obey is that each shell of any atom always tries to have exactly four pairs of electrons.

Let us look at the atomic structure of quartz, made of silicon (Si), and oxygen (O). In Figure 8a only the electrons in the outermost shell of each atom are shown. We see that the silicon atom has four electrons in its outermost shell, and the oxygen atom has six. Now if these two atoms attempt to share their outermost electrons, as in Figure 8b, remembering that the outermost shell likes to have no

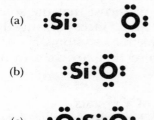

Figure 8   The formation of a quartz molecule

more than eight electrons, we discover that we have two extra electrons. Since we cannot have extra electrons in a covalent type of bond, the silicon solves the problem rather neatly by attracting to itself a second oxygen atom, as shown in Figure 8c. In this case, the silicon now shares two of its electrons with one oxygen, and two of its electrons with a second oxygen, and in turn shares six electrons with each oxygen. Now, if we count up the number of atoms of each element that has combined to make an electron balance and write them as a ratio, in this case one atom of silicon to two atoms of oxygen, we discover that we have also derived the chemical formula for quartz, which is written SiO_2. So, when you see a chemical formula written for a particular mineral, this is the actual process that the formula describes — the ratios between the number of atoms of each element that share electrons.

Having discovered how atoms attach themselves to one another, we can now begin to examine the patterns they then form and how these patterns build up to form crystals. But what is a crystal? The text book definition is that a crystal is the regular polyhedral form, bonded by smooth faces, which is assumed by a chemical compound, under the action of its interatomic forces, when passing, under suitable conditions, from the state of a liquid or gas to that of a solid.

What this means in simple terms is that a crystal is characterized, first, by its definite internal structure and, second, by its external form; that its atoms are attracted together in regular patterns; that the solid produced by these patterns has flat faces arranged in a precise geometric form; and that its atoms are supplied from a liquid or a gas (where they are free to move into their proper positions).

Internal Structure of Crystals

A geometrically regular arrangement of points in space is called a space lattice. At the left of Figure 9 is shown one kind of space lattice. The points have been connected to make their locations obvious. Now, imagine gold atoms have been placed in a space lattice in such a way that the nucleus of each atom is centred on a lattice point. The result is a portion of a crystal lattice of gold, and is shown at the right of Figure 9. A crystal lattice may be thought of as a space lattice in which the points are occupied by atoms or ions. The arrangement of atoms or ions in a crystal lattice repeats regularly in three dimensions, up to the physical boundaries of each single crystal.

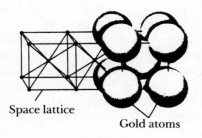

Space lattice

Gold atoms

Figure 9

In order to simplify the description of a crystal lattice, it is useful to describe the unit cell of that lattice. A unit cell is a small portion of the lattice which can be used to construct the entire lattice by moving the unit cell according to certain rules. Before we can see how this is done, let us first look at a two dimensional figure: the *net*.

A net is a regular repeating series of points on a flat surface. Figure 10 shows a net. An obvious choice for a unit cell for the net is the square, shown in the upper left

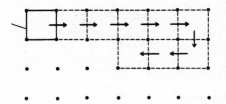

Figure 10   A net generated from a square cell

hand corner of Figure 10. The unit cell can be used to produce the entire net by moving it a distance equal to its own length to the right, and also parallel to that edge down. The figure shows eight such movements, after which a total of fourteen additional points of the net have been generated from the starting four of the unit cell.

Now if we place some object at each point of the net, we have something which corresponds to a crystal lattice, but only in two dimensions. In Figure 11 an atom has been

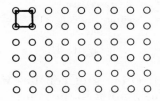

Figure 11   Crystal lattice

placed at each net point. The result can be completely described by simply specifying the nature of the unit cell: a square with an atom at each corner. Now, we can generalize into three dimensions. Figure 12 shows one unit cell of a simple cubic lattice. It is a cube with a point at each corner only, and is called the simple cubic unit cell. There are two other types of cubic space lattices, and the unit cells of each are shown in Figure 13.

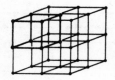

Figure 12   Cubic space lattice with unit cell

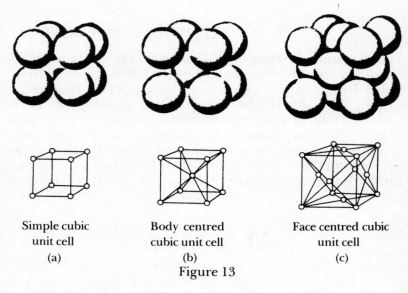

Simple cubic	Body centred	Face centred cubic
unit cell	cubic unit cell	unit cell
(a)	(b)	(c)

Figure 13

The body-centred cubic unit cell has in addition to the eight corner points a point in the centre of the cube body. The face-centred cubic unit cell has a point in the centre of each face, as well as the corner points. For each unit cell, both a ball and stick model is shown and a representation of how the cell would look if an atom were placed at each point.

In the following chapter we shall look at many crystal forms, all built around only a handful of unit cells — and only one unit cell per crystal at that. Let's now look at some of the cubic unit cells, and see how we can get different external shapes from them.

Beginning with the simple cubic unit cell, in Figure 14,

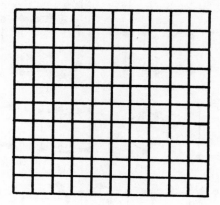

Figure 14   Cubes stacked to form a cubic crystal

we can stack them up to build a crystal that is a cube. In Figure 15, we can also stack them up to build an octahedron.

Figure 15   Cubes stacked to form an octahedral crystal

In the body-centred cubic unit cell (Figure 13b), the atom in the centre of the basic cube can itself become the corner of another such cube, and such a stacking can produce a dodecahedron. With the face-centred cube (13c), each atom can also be the corner of another such cube —

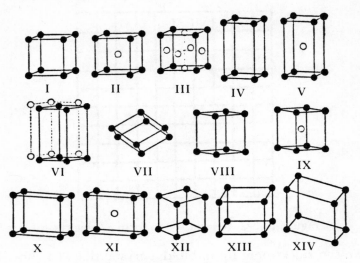

Figure 16   Bravais unit cells

the forms yielded by this combination are the more complex forms of the Cubic System (see Chapter 3).

In 1848, the French scientist A. Bravais showed that there were only fourteen fundamentally different ways of regularly arranging points in space. These fourteen space lattices, often called Bravais lattices, fall into six sets corresponding to the six crystal systems. The unit cells of each of these six sets is shown in Figure 16. Note that these unit cells differ from each other in the angles between their faces and/or the lengths of their edges.

The space lattice is composed of points and the lines on the drawings mainly help the eyes to connect the points; but in the crystal lattice, where the points are filled by atoms or ions, in most instances the lines will represent the bonding between the atoms. In a crystal lattice each point of the space lattice is occupied by the same unit, either an atom or an ion, but never both.

There are two main factors that determine which particular unit cell will form — packing, and atomic diameter. The term packing refers to the way the atoms fill the space available. Two different types of packing are shown in Figure 17. Layers of atoms in hexagonal packing

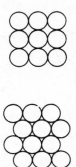

Figure 17   Two types of packing

are shown in Figure 18. In many types of minerals, the atoms arrange themselves in such layers. But in both types of layering, either cubic or hexagonal, the spheres do not completely fill the space and a hole is left between the atoms. The type of layering will determine the shape of

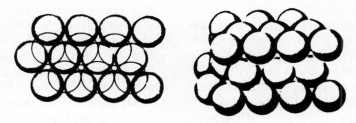

Figure 18   Atoms in hexagonal packing

the hole. The arrangement of atoms to produce such holes is shown in Figure 19. It is into these holes that atoms of a smaller diameter will fit, but *which* atom will depend on its diameter and outer shell filling (therefore determining the chemical composition of that particular mineral).

There is one type of crystal that has not been covered, and this is the crystal of a pure metal. These do not occur often in nature in single crystals and, with the possible exception of copper crystals, it is unlikely that the user of crystal energy will have much contact with them. Metallic crystals have significantly different properties when energy passes

TOP VIEW

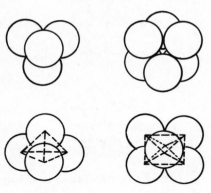

Tetrahedral hole   Octaheldral hole
Figure 19

through them, which make them a great deal less usable as spiritual instruments. Figure 20 shows a crystal of copper metal. Each unit occupying the lattice points of this metal is a positive ion. Each copper ion can be considered to have lost two electrons and to have contributed them to an electron cloud which permeates the entire lattice. These electrons are not bound to any one atom or even to a pair of atoms, but move freely through the entire crystal, and are therefore called free electrons. They are also referred to as an electron gas; in a typical metal, there is a mutual attraction between the electron gas and the ions.

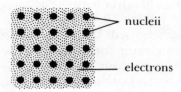

Figure 20   A metal crystal with electron gas

This stabilizes the structure, but at the same time allows it to be greatly distorted without falling apart. Thus most metals are relatively soft, and easily deformed. In certain metals, such as tungsten and chromium, the metallic bonding is supplemented by covalent bonds between adjacent atoms, giving these metals their greater hardness. These bonds tend to keep the structure locked in place, preventing easy deformation. The melting points of metals vary greatly because of this variability of bonding. Sodium metal, for example, melts at 98° centigrade, while tungsten melts at 3410° centigrade.

The free electrons in a metal give rise to its electrical conductivity. Electrons can readily be added to the electron gas at one end of a piece of metal and simultaneously withdrawn from the other end, which is how electrical current flows along a wire. The characteristic lustre of a metal is also caused by the free electrons. The unbound electrons at the surface of the metal absorb and re-radiate light which strikes the surface. As this happens, the smooth metal surface reflects light completely at all angles, giving metals their particular sheen.

To sum up, if we take the analogy of the unit cell as a building block, the actual shape of the structures that we build with it will be determined by the shape of the block itself. Thus, if we have a cubic building block, the crystal forms built from it will be those that relate to the shape and symmetry of the cube. We can also look at this in reverse order, and see that the shape of the crystal will reflect its internal structure, and we can make a good guess about the shape of the building blocks simply from the shape of the crystal. Once again, we see the microcosm reflecting the macrocosm, and vice versa; and we see that from the tiniest structure of the atom to the very universe itself, there is an order and a simplicity which simply repeats and repeats, and that order and simplicity is the basic essence of creation.

In the next chapter we examine the external forms of crystals, and their relationship to the fourteen basic building blocks just described.

3.

Crystals and Their Forms

It is only within about the last hundred years that man has begun to understand how and why crystals grow. Much of the knowledge we now have about crystals has been dependent on other sciences, such as chemistry and physics, providing us with the method and means of study. Crystals are, of course, naturally occurring chemical compounds, and the ordinary laws of chemistry and physics apply equally to crystals as to some formula bubbling away in the laboratory.

The most fundamental concepts of crystal formation are based on the atom and the behaviour of its electrons. And yet, the atom itself was not accepted as a reality until about 1803, the electron was not discovered until 1898, and the neutron was not discovered until the 1930s. Thus, we can see the monumental amount of work, supported by some extraordinarily intuitive insights about the nature of matter, that has led to the modern study of minerology.

The history of this study is covered in a later chapter, but it is important to realize that until the turn of the century the study of crystals was based almost entirely on their physical forms, which led to some remarkably correct guesses about their internal structure.

Before we go further into the study of forms, the difference between a crystal and a mineral should be made clear. A mineral is a substance that occurs in nature; it is inorganic, has a definite chemical makeup, and, if conditions are ideal, forms crystals that are characteristic of that mineral. From our previous definition of a crystal, we remember that a crystal has a definite atomic structure and flat faces arranged in a geometric pattern. From these two definitions, it is clear that a crystal is always a mineral but that not all minerals are crystals.

If a mineral has no external crystal form, it is said to be *massive*. If it has a regular atomic structure, it is said to be *crystalline*. If it has a more or less distinct crystalline structure that cannot be resolved into individual crystals, it is said to be *crypto-crystalline*.

A look at the mineral quartz demonstrates all of these terms. Quartz is first a mineral because it occurs in nature, is inorganic and has a definite chemical composition (one atom of silicon to two atoms of oxygen, written SiO_2). The type of the mineral quartz known as rose quartz is massive in form, because it does not usually have flat faces; but it *does* have a regular atomic structure, making it crystalline.

The type of the mineral quartz known as *agate* is also a massive form, composed of millions of microscopic crystalline bits, but which are not individual crystals. It is crypto-crystalline.

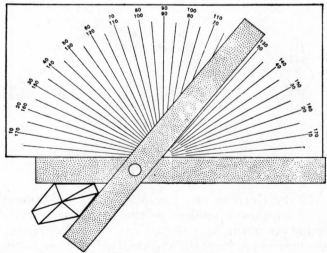

Figure 21   Contact goniometer

It is only when we come to varieties of the mineral quartz such as rock crystal, amethyst, citrine, etc., that we find *crystals*; that is, although they are chemically identical to the massive forms (SiO_2), they take forms that have a regular atomic structure and flat faces arranged in geometric patterns.

One of the earliest discoveries about crystals was that the angles between adjacent corresponding faces in a given crystal are the same for every crystal of that mineral and are characteristic of that mineral. This is called the Law of Constancy of Interfacial Angles. To measure these angles, instruments called goniometers were used, which ranged from a simple contact goniometer (Figure 21) to complex and highly accurate reflecting goniometers, resembling surveyors' instruments. Using data from instruments such as these, and the newly forming theories regarding atomic structure, by the turn of the century certain predictions were being made regarding the spacing of atoms in the crystal structures.

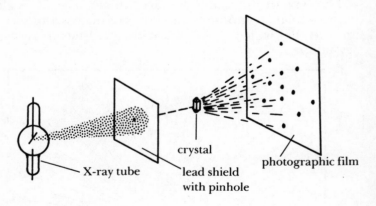

Figure 22   Laüe apparatus

In 1912 the German physicist Max von Laüe pointed out that the supposed positions of the atoms in a crystal are spaced at about the right distance to allow them to serve as the elements of a three-dimensional diffraction grating for X-rays. Shortly afterwards, an experiment was performed shooting a beam of X-rays at a crystal of copper sulphate ($CuSO_4$), which verified that the predicted diffraction (bending) actually took place. This was the birth of X-ray crystallography.

Figure 22 shows an apparatus used to obtain a diffraction pattern. A beam of monochromatic (single wavelength) X-rays is shot at a crystal and the emerging diffracted beams register on a sheet of photographic film. The resulting pattern of spots is called a Laüe pattern (Figure 23) and depends on the relative locations of the atoms in the crystal. It was found that not only does the symmetry of the dots exactly duplicate the symmetry of the crystal but also that the size of the dots corresponds to the sizes of the faces which appear on the crystal. In other words, the major faces on any given crystal appear as the largest dots, etc. It was also discovered that the angular relationship between the dots on the photograph is exactly equivalent to the angular relationship between the faces that appear on the crystal.

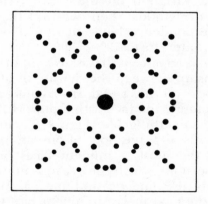

Figure 23   Laüe photography

In 1913 William and Lawrence Bragg showed that diffraction of X-rays can be imagined to occur as if the X-rays were reflected by layers of atoms in a crystal, much as light is reflected by a mirror. They showed that there is a very simple relationship between the distance between the layers, the wavelength of the X-radiation and the angle

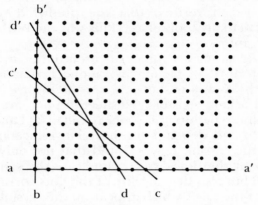

Figure 24   Crystal point system

of diffraction. Thus, it is possible to measure the actual distances between atoms. There are several other methods of studying the internal form of crystals using X-rays, but they are all a variation on these two basic principles. Through these methods, then, we find that there is an absolute correspondence between inner form (the unit cell) and the outer forms.

There is one last concept that is also important, and that is the relationship between the density of atoms and the faces that appear on the crystal. If we could cut through a crystal and examine the face with a powerful microscope, we might see something like Figure 24, in which each point represents the position of an atom. We would discover that the most prominent faces on the crystal would be those along which the greatest number of atoms occur — in this case, line *a-a'* and line *b-b'*. We would also discover that the next most prominent face would correspond to the second greatest density of atoms (line *c-c'*) and the third most prominent would have the third greatest concentration (line *d-d'*), and so forth.

Classification of Crystal Forms
In the early part of the nineteenth century atomic theory was in its infancy; the science of chemistry was likewise just beginning, and a large percentage of the chemical ele-

ments was still unknown. Not only that, but many minerals are difficult to break down chemically into their constituent elements. Without a chemical basis to study crystals, imagine the bewilderment of a mineralogist sitting at a desk with perhaps hundreds or even thousands of different crystals, trying to decide some sort of a rational basis for relating one crystal to another. Formerly, one of the usual ways of categorizing crystals was by colour; but as we can clearly see from Figure 25, the crystals of three different minerals, all red in colour, bear little or no resemblance to one another. It fell to an American mineralogist, James White Dana, to propose a system of classifying crystals by their geometric properties. How this system came about may perhaps be best described in an imaginary scenario (with apologies to Mr Dana).

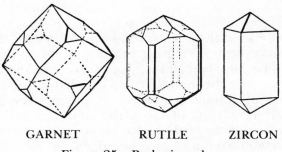

GARNET   RUTILE   ZIRCON

Figure 25   Red minerals

We might well imagine Mr Dana with a huge box of crystals of all sizes, shapes and colours. He may have picked up a cubic crystal of the mineral pyrite, and reflected on its perfect geometric form, the cube being the most perfect of all forms occurring in the mineral kingdom. Perhaps he held the cube between his thumb and forefinger, with each finger centred on opposing cubic faces. He may then have discovered that if he rotated the cube through ninety degrees the cube appears exactly as it did before it was rotated — in other words, that another square face was facing towards him. He may further have noticed that if he did this again, he got another identical face in the same position. This process is

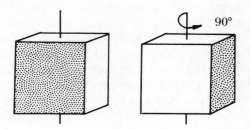

Figure 26   Axis of rotation in the cube

shown in Figure 26. If he rotated it through 360°, there would have been four repetitions of identical square faces. If he held the same cube by another set of two faces, and did the same thing, he would have again observed a repetition of four square faces. Using the last two sets of parallel faces (a cube is three sets of parallel faces at right angles to each other), he would have discovered the same thing. Since he was rotating this crystal on an imaginary axis, and because he had four repetitions of identical faces as he rotated it through 360°, he decided to call this a 4–fold Axis of Rotation. And since it happened through three different pairs of faces, the cube was said to have three, 4–fold Axes of Rotation. He may then have picked up an octahedron, and discovered that it also has three, 4–fold Axes of Rotation (Figure 27), and likewise the

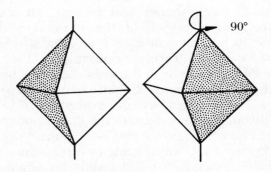

Figure 27   Axis of symmetry in an octahedron

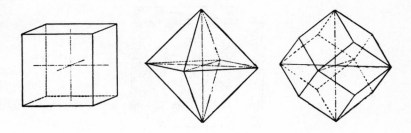

Figure 28

dodecahedron. These three are seen in Figure 28.

In studying these three forms he also made another interesting discovery — that if you cut a cube exactly down the middle you get two halves that are a mirror image of one another. Likewise, if you cut a cube vertically or horizontally the same situation occurs. Since in geometry such an operation is said to be putting a *plane* through a solid, and since the two halves on either side of the plane are absolutely symmetrical, these are called Planes of Symmetry. The principal Planes of Symmetry of the cube are shown in Figure 29. Planes placed diagonally in the cube produce the same result; that is, each plane placed through the cube produces two halves that are mirror

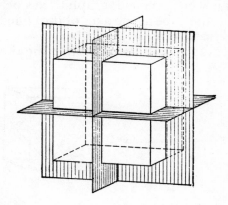

Figure 29   Principle planes of symmetry in the cube

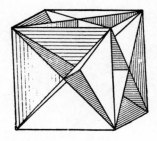

Figure 30　Diagonal symmetry planes in the cube

images of each other. These are shown in Figure 30.

In placing planes of symmetry through the octahedron and dodecahedron, identical results were found; thus, from the standpoint of geometry, the cube, octahedron and dodecahedron are geometrically related. One other important observation was made about these three ·geometric forms, which was the axes of symmetry were all of equal length and at 90° to one another. Although these are axes of symmetry we must also remember that the external form is exactly representative of the internal form, and therefore that the geometric relationships of the symmetry axes are also exactly equivalent to the geometric relationship of the atomic arrangement. Therefore, geometric axes also become the crystallographic axes, and all crystals whose crystallographic axes bear the same relationship to the cube as the axes of the cube fall into the same geometric system as the cube.

In crystallography, this then becomes the first system of

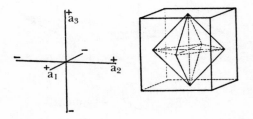

Figure 31　Isometric axes

classification, called the *Isometric* (a latin word meaning equal measure) system, also called the *Regular* or *Cubic* system. All crystals which have crystallographic axes of equal length at 90° to each other fall into the Isometric system. The Isometric axes are shown in Figure 31. All crystals in the Isometric system also have a cubic unit cell (numbers I, II or III Figure 16). In any individual crystal, any or all of the basic forms may be present, in various combinations (Figures 32–36).

Figure 32   Octahedron and cube

Figure 33   Cube and octahedron

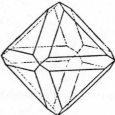

Figure 34   Octahedron and dodecahedron

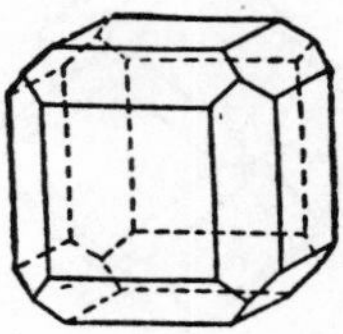

Figure 35   Cube, dodecahedron and dodecahedron

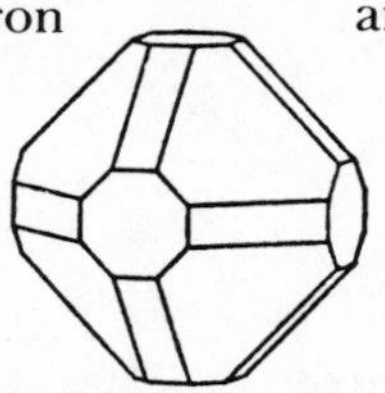

Figure 36   Cube, dodecahedron and octahedron

Sub-divisions in each system can also be made based on the number of symmetry planes, although the unit cells are still the same and the crystallographic axes maintain their basic relationship to one another. Other forms that appear in the Isometric system are shown in Figures 37–46. Crystals of two different minerals showing the multiplicity

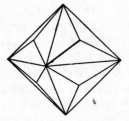

Figure 37   Trisoctrahedron

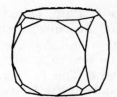

Figure 38   Trisoctahedron
and cube

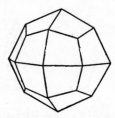

Figure 39   Trapezogedron

Figure 40   Trapezogedron
and octahedron

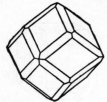

Figure 41   Dodecahedron
and trapezohedron

Figure 42   Pyritahedron

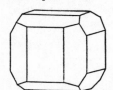

Figure 43   Pyritahedron
and cube

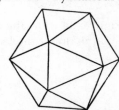

Figure 44   Octahedron and
pyritahedron

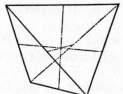

Figure 45   Tetrahedron

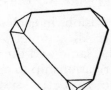

Figure 46   Tetrahedron
and dodecahedron

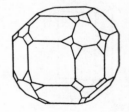

Figure 47   Sphalerite   Figure 48   Boracite

of forms that can occur are shown in Figures 47 and 48.
Having taken quite a few crystals from his box and placed
them in the Isometric system, Mr Dana would then have
turned to the remaining pile and selected another group
of crystals, discovering that, in this particular group, the
crystallographic axes were still at 90° to one another, but in
this instance, one axis was longer or shorter than the other
two, which were still of equal length. In this system, the
axes of equal length are labelled *a-a'* as in the Isometric
system, but the axis of differing length is called the 'C' axis,
(Figure 49). This system is called the *Tetragonal* system.

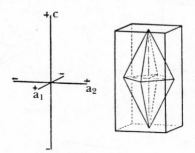

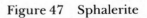

Figure 49   Tetragonal axes

The unit cells of the Tetragonal system are cells IV and V,
Figure 16.It is easily seen that the unit cells of the
Tetragonal system are square in section, and elongated.
You will notice that Tetragonal crystals have the same
appearance. As in the Isometric system, the Tetragonal
system is sub-divided into different classes, once again

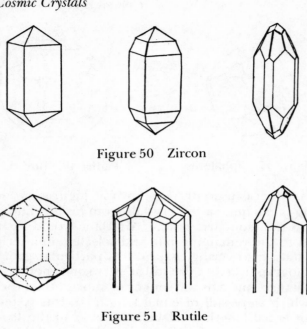

Figure 50   Zircon

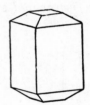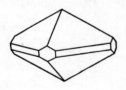

Figure 51   Rutile

Figure 52   Vesuvianite

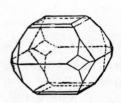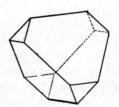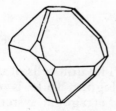

Figure 54   Tetrahedrite

Figure 53   Wulfenite   Figure 55   Chalcopyrite

based on symmetry. Figures 50–55 are typical crystals appearing in the Tetragonal system.

All crystal systems beyond the Isometric system have a 'C' axis, and it is on the basis of this axis that crystal faces are given particular names. A crystal face parallel to the 'C' axis is called a *prism* face, and such faces are generally rectangular in appearance (see Figure 56). Faces which cut through the 'C' axis are called pyramid faces, and they are often triangular in appearance. If pyramid faces are present at differing angles to the 'C' axis, all but the last face may have their points 'cut off' (Figure 56). Faces that are perpendicular to the 'C' axis are called *pinacoids*. The combination of faces that makes up the 'point' of a crystal is called the *termination*. Pinacoid faces are shown at the very 'point' of the crystal termination shown in Figure 56. If a crystal has 'points' at both ends it is said to be *double terminated*.

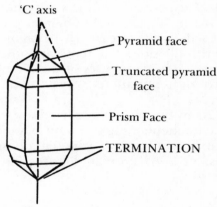

'C' axis

Pyramid face

Truncated pyramid face

Prism Face

TERMINATION

Figure 56   Faces of crystals

The next system Mr Dana may have studied was the *Hexagonal* system, made up of unit cells VI and VII (Figure 16) and having four axes instead of three. In this instance, there are three horizontal axes of equal lengths in a common plane, and intersecting at angles of 60°, and a fourth, a vertical axis at right angles to them (Figure 57).

The Hexagonal system is further subdivided into two different divisions, the hexagonal division, and the rhom-

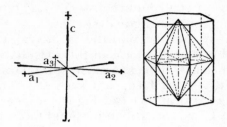

Figure 57   Hexagonal axes

bohedral division. The rhombohedral division is also called the *Trigonal system* by some writers, and in some text books is listed as a separate system from the Hexagonal system. This is seen mainly in European text books, and gives a total of seven rather than six systems as described by Dana. The writer believes that it is rightfully a part of the Hexagonal system, as the hexagonal axes still apply (Figure 58); in addition, many crystals, such as quartz crystals, which are clearly hexagonal in form, are included in this division. The temptation is to try for seven systems based on the esoterics of the Number 7, but these are the sort of temptations which often lead us further from reality.

As in the other systems, there are further division into classes, depending again on symmetry. Crystals of various minerals in the hexagonal division of the Hexagonal system are shown in Figures 59 and 60.

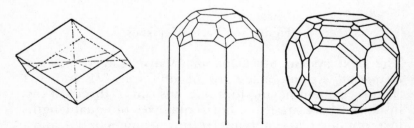

Figure 58   Rhombohedron   Figure 60   Apatite

Figure 59   Beryl

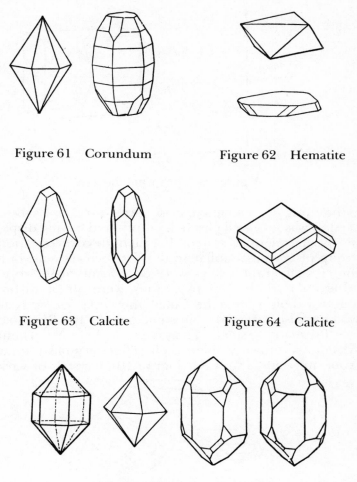

Figure 61   Corundum

Figure 62   Hematite

Figure 63   Calcite

Figure 64   Calcite

Figure 65   Quartz crystals

The rhombohedral division of the Hexagonal system is likewise sub-divided into various classes, and crystals of the various mineral crystallizing in this division are shown in Figures 61–65. As can be seen from the crystal drawings, most of the minerals traditionally considered as hexagonal occur in this division.

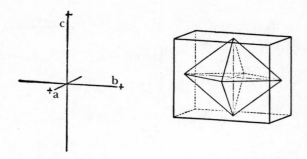

Figure 66   Orthorhombic axes

Continuing our imaginary scenario, Mr Dana's box of crystals was now well past half empty, and having disposed of the Hexagonal system he then discovered another group of crystals, similar to the first two systems, in that the crystallographic axes were once again at 90° to each other, but in this instance, they were all of different lengths. This system he called the *Orthorhombic* system, which is also referred to in some texts as the Rhombic or the Prismatic system. The axes of the Orthorhombic system are shown in Figure 66. These crystals are made from unit cells X and XI (Figure 16). Crystals of various

Figure 67   Barite

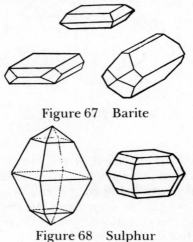

Figure 68   Sulphur

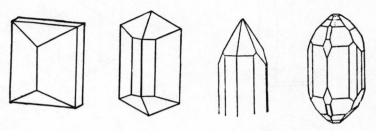

Figure 69   Staurolite   Figure 70   Topaz

minerals which form in this system are shown in Figures 67–70.

Mr Dana's box was now nearly empty, but still contained a significant number of crystals of one very large mineral group, the feldspars. Feldspars are the most numerous of all crystals on the Earth and are principally made either of potassium and silica, or of sodium and silica. Most of the feldspars crystallize in the fifth system, and a few in the sixth.

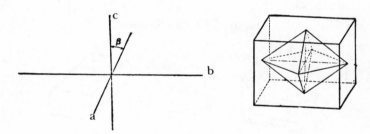

Figure 71   Monoclinic axes

Crystals in the fifth system have the characteristic of three crystal axes of differing length, with the a and b axes lying in the same plane, but the plane of the axes is tilted in relation to the 'C' axis (Figure 71). This system is called the *Monoclinic* system. Minerals that crystallize in the Monoclinic system, and their forms, are shown in Figures 72 and 73. These crystals form from unit cells XII and XIII (Figure 16).

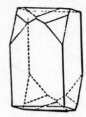

Figure 72   Pyroxene

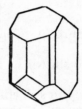

Figure 73   Orthoclase

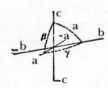

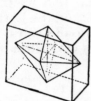

Figure 74   Triclinic axes

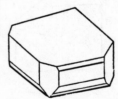

Figure 75   Rhodonite

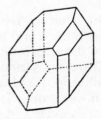

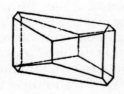

Figure 76   Axianite

Figure 77   Albite

The last crystal system is called the *Triclinic* system and has three axes of different lengths. None of the angles between any of the axes are right angles. The triclinic axes are shown in Figure 74 and typical triclinic crystals are shown in figures 75–77. The triclinic unit cell is cell XIV (Figure 16).

Twin Crystals
Another group of crystals is made up of various representatives of each of the six different crystal systems. These are called Twin Crystals, and are made by two or more identical crystals growing together in certain patterns.

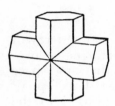
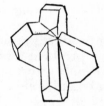
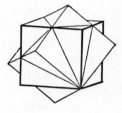

Figure 78   Staurolite   Figure 79   Flourite

The first type of such twins are called *penetration twins*. In a penetration twin, illustrated by the minerals fluorite and staurolite in Figures 78 and 79, where two or more complete crystals appear actually to penetrate each other. In fact, these crystals tend to have a common centre and have simply grown from this centre in two separate yet intermingled growths.

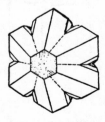
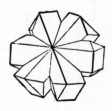

Figure 80   Chrysoberyl   Figure 81   Staurolite

It is also possible to have repeated twinning along common faces of several crystals, giving rise to circular appearing crystals, called *cyclic twins,* such as that of chrysoberyl, illustrated in Figure 80, and staurolite, Figure 81. Other twins are shown in Figures 82 and 83.

Figure 82   Gypsum   Figure 83   Feldspar

The mineral quartz also produces an interesting array of twin crystals. Quartz also produces another type of twin that appears to be two crystals growing in the same space and that also appears to be only one crystal. This type of twin is called a right-hand crystal, as opposed to the 'normal' quartz crystal, called a left-hand crystal. These names derive from the tendency of the tetrahedral-shaped quartz molecules to arrange themselves in spiral patterns. In the left-handed crystal the spirals turn to the left, but in the right-handed crystal, the spirals turn to *both* the left and right.

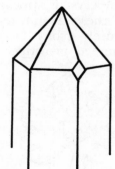

(a) Left-hand crystal   (b) right-hand crystal

Figure 84   Quartz

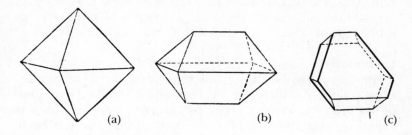

Figure 85   Distorted octahedrons

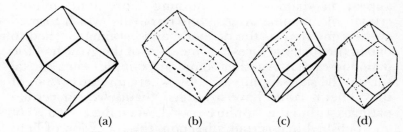

Figure 86   Distorted dodecahedrons

There are no quartz crystals where the spirals turn *only* to the right. This is an area where there is a great deal of confusion by esoteric writers about crystals, and is discussed in Chapter 13. The right-hand crystal is identified by the presence of a lozenge-shaped face(s) present to the right of the largest pyramid face of the crystal (Figure 84). If the face appears to the left of the pyramid face, it is a left-hand crystal. Most quartz crystals are mixtures of both.

Distorted Forms
Crystals of the forms illustrated throughout this chapter are idealized forms and occur in nature only under very ideal conditions. In Figures 85 and 86 the idealized form of the crystal is shown, along with distorted crystals, more commonly found in nature. It must be remembered, though, that the laws of symmetry by which the crystal systems are derived apply to the *position* of their faces, and

not to their actual dimensions. Therefore, even a distorted crystal still represents the basic elements of symmetry as much as an ideal crystal.

Inclusions

There may also be numerous types of internal imperfections, many of which are not visible to the naked eye. One of the most common types of internal imperfections is called an *inclusion*, which is defined as any foreign body enclosed within the crystal. These are extremely common and may take the form of crystals of other minerals, bubbles of gas, or liquid. The so-called black spots which appear in diamonds are nothing more than minute crystals of the minerals graphite or olivine, which formed at the same time as the diamond and became attached to one of the forming faces at some stage of the growth of the diamond crystal. Another common example is in a crystal such as the star sapphire or ruby, where minute crystals of the mineral rutile have arranged themselves in certain patterns within the sapphire crystal; when the crystal is cut and polished in a certain direction, the reflection of light from these tiny particles of rutile forms a star pattern.

Classification of Minerals

While crystals are classified by their geometry, minerals are classified by their chemical composition. Remember that a crystal is always a mineral (and, according to the definition, characteristic of that mineral), but minerals do not always form crystals. Our definition of minerals stated that minerals were always of a definite chemical composition and it is thus that we classify them.

SCHEME OF CLASSIFICATION

   I NATIVE ELEMENTS

  II SULPHIDES, SELENIDES, TELLURIDES, AR-SENIDES, ANTIMONIDES.

 III *Sulpho-salts* — SULPHARSENITES, SULPHANT-IMONITES, SULPHO-BISMU-THITES.

 IV *Haloids* — CHLORIDES, BROMIDES, IODIDES; FLUORIDES.

V OXIDES.

VI *Oxygen Salts.*
    1. CARBONATES.
    2. SILICATES, TITANITES.
    3. NIOBATES, TANTALATES.
    4. PHOSPHATES, ARSENATES, VANADATES;
       ANTIMONATES; NITRATES.
    5. BORATES, URANATES.
    6. SULPHATES, CHROMATES, TELLURATES.
    7. TUNGSTATES, MOLYBDATES.

VII *Salts of Organic Acids:* OXALATES, MELLATES, ETC.

VIII HYDROCARBON COMPOUNDS.

The first group of minerals is simply called the *Native Elements.* These are elements that occur in nature uncombined with other elements. Typical examples would be gold, silver, platinum, sulphur, copper, and carbon (in the form of diamond and graphite). Crystals of some of these minerals are shown in Figures 87–90.

Figure 87   Diamond crystals

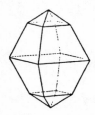

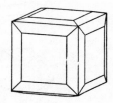

Figure 88 Sulphur   Figure 89   Gold   Figure 90   Copper

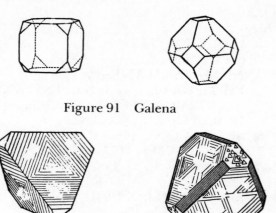

Figure 91   Galena

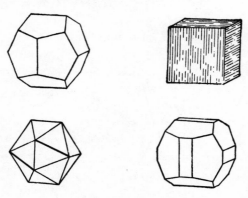

Figure 92   Sphalerite

In Group II, the most commonly encountered group of minerals would be from the *Sulphides*. This group is chemically simple, involving nothing more than a metal (X) combined with sulphur (X)S. Crystals commonly encountered are those of galena (PbS), where the 'X' metal is lead (Figure 91); sphalerite (ZnS), where the 'X' metal is zinc (Figure 92); pyrite (FeS_2), where the 'X' metal is iron (Figure 93) and which crystallizes in the Isometric system; and marcasite, chemically identical to pyrite, which crystallizes in the Orthorhombic system.

Figure 93   Pyrite

Pyrite and marcasite also give an excellent example of how a mineral is categorized not only by its chemical composition, but also by its crystal form (remembering that in the definition, there was a characteristic crystal form for each mineral). If we have two minerals of the same chemical composition but forming in different crystal systems, they are in fact two different minerals and are given different names. This same situation occurs in other mineral groups, and will be pointed out as we go along.

Group III, the *Sulpho-salts*, are unlikely to be encountered as large single crystals, and are not commonly available.

Group IV, the *Haloids*, are formed from a metal combined with one of the halogen chemical group — chlorine, bromine, iodine or fluorine.

In this group we would find minerals such as halite (rock salt — NaCl) and fluorite, also called fluor spar (CaF_2). Crystals of halite and fluorite are shown in Figures 94 and 95.

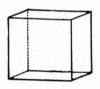 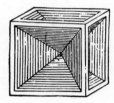

Figure 94   Halite

 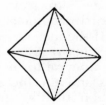

Figure 95   Fluorite

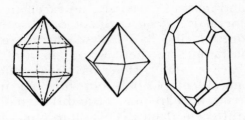

Figure 96   Quartz crystals

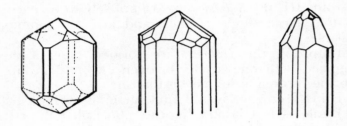

Figure 97   Rutile

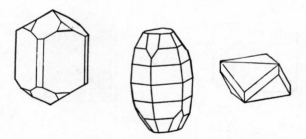

Figure 98   Corundum crystals

The next group, group V, is formed by the combination of some particular metal (X) with oxygen and is called the *Oxides*. If the metal is silicon (Si) the mineral formed then becomes quartz (SiO_2: Figure 96). If the metal is titanium (Ti) the mineral formed is rutile (TiO_2: Figure 97). If the oxygens and the metals combine in a slightly different proportion, then we get minerals such as corundum (the red variety of which is ruby, and the blue variety sapphire), where the 'X' metal is aluminium, giving the

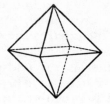 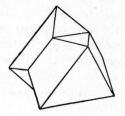

Figure 99   Spinel crystals

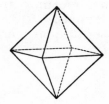 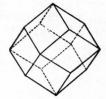

Figure 100   Magnetite crystals

Figure 101   Hematite crystals

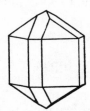 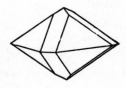

Figure 102   Cassiterite crystals

chemical formula Al_2O_3: (Figure 98). Other common minerals which form this group are spinel, magnetite, (Lodestone), and Hematite. Also included is the oxide of tin, cassiterite (Figures 99–102).

Although in total volume of minerals, the feldspars are the most predominant on the Earth, quartz has the greatest number of varieties and is probably the second most common mineral on the Earth. Mineralogists divide the varieties of quartz into two separate sections — vitreous (meaning that each of the varieties has a glassy appearance), and cryptocrystalline, meaning that it is made up of microscopic quartz crystals.

Listed below are the various types of quartz in each of the two groups with its description:

ROCK CRYSTAL

Colourless quartz or nearly so.

ASTERIATED: STAR QUARTZ

Contains inclusions of submicroscopic needles of some other mineral, showing a star when polished.

AMETHYST

Clear purple or bluish violet — colouring probably due to ferric iron.

ROSE

Rose red or pink, commonly massive. Colour perhaps due to titanium.

CITRINE

Yellow in colour resembling yellow topaz.

SMOKY: CAIRNGORMSTONE

Smoky yellow to dark smoky brown, varying to brownish black. The name MORION is the proper name for nearly black varieties.

MILKY

Milk white and nearly opaque.

SAGENITIC

Enclosing needle-like crystals of rutile, or black tourmaline; or other minerals such as asbestos, hornblende, epidote.

CAT'S EYE

Exhibits opalescence but without prismatic colours; Tiger Eye is also a variety. The gemstone variety of Cat's Eye is a variety of chrysoberyl.

AVENTURINE

Spangled with scales of mica, hematite or other minerals.

CHALCEDONY

Having the lustre nearly of wax; transparent to translucent, colour white, greyish, blue, pale brown to dark brown, black; also shades, with other names.

CARNELIAN, SARD

A clear red chalcedony, pale to deep in shades; also brownish red to brown.

CHRYSOPRASE

An apple green chalcedony, the colour due to nickel oxide.

PRASE

Translucent and dull leek green.

PLASMA

Rather bright green, sometimes nearly emerald green. Heliotrope or bloodstone is the same stone essentially, with small spots of red jasper, looking like drops of blood.

AGATE

A layered chalcedony. The colours are either banded, irregularly clouded, or due to visible impurities such as in moss agate, which has brown or green moss-like forms distributed through the mass. The bands are delicate parallel lines of white, pale and dark brown, blueish and other shades. They are sometimes straight, but are often wavy or zigzag, and occasionally circular. There is also agatized wood — natural wood replaced by agate.

ONYX

Like agate and consisting of layers of different colours, but the layers are in even lines and the banding straight.

SARDONYX

Like onyx in structure but includes layers of carnelian (sard) along with others of white or brown.

FLINT

Somewhat like chalcedony, but more opaque and of dull colours. The flint of chalk formations consists largely of the remains of diatoms, sponges and others of marine production.

JASPER

Impure opaque coloured quartz; commonly red — also yellow, dark green and greyish blue.

TOUCHSTONE: BASANITE

A velvet black siliceous stone or flinty jasper, used on account of its hardness and black colour for trying the purity of precious metals.

There are also other varieties of quartz, but these are the most common and the names that the friends of the mineral kingdom are likely to encounter.

Another type of silica similar to quartz but made up of layers of microscopic balls of silica and containing water in the structure, is *opal*. There are many varieties of opal, but the most common are *precious opal*, exhibiting a play of delicate colours and *fire opal*, which is hyacinth red to honey yellow, with fire-like reflections. The majority of opal is *common opal*, which is usually transparent to translucent, and milky white, yellow or olive green in colour. There are other varieties of opal but these are the most common.

Within Group VI, the *Oxygen Salts*, an important group

is the *Carbonates,* in which group carbon and oxygen combine with an 'X' metal. In this group, if the 'X' metal is iron, the mineral becomes Siderite ($FeCO_3$), or if the metal is zinc the mineral becomes Smithsonite ($ZnCO_3$).

Still in the Carbonate group, the 'X' metal may be calcium, which combines with carbon and oxygen ($CaCO_3$) to form either calcite (Figure 103), or the mineral aragonite. Chemically, both minerals are identical, but in calcite the crystals form in the rhombohedral division of the Hexagonal system and aragonite crystals form in the Orthorhombic system. This is, once again, an example of how identical chemical substances are classed as different minerals when their crystals fall into different crystal systems.

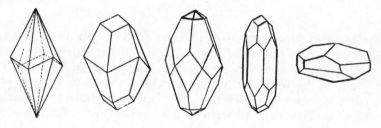

Figure 103   Calcite crystals

In Group VI, the *Phosphates* are of significance to the human body, bone tissue being principally made of the mineral apatite, as is tooth enamel. Apatite is made from calcium and fluorine combined with phosphorus and oxygen. Crystals of apatite are shown in Figure 104.

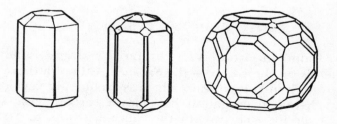

Figure 104   Apatite

Another phosphate mineral is an iron/magnesium aluminium phosphate called lazulite, crystals of which, when dispersed in calcite, form the rock lapis-lazuli. Another phosphate gem mineral is turquoise. It is usually massive in form but crystals are occasionally found.

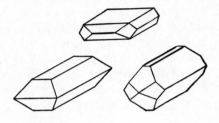

Figure 105   Barite

Within the *Sulphates*, Group VI, we find the mineral barite, also known as barytes. This is the metal barium combined with sulphur and oxygen ($BaSO_4$), crystals of which are shown in Figure 105. Gypsum, the crystalline variety of which is known as selenite, is also a sulphate, but with water in the crystal structure. Crystals of selenite are shown in Figure 106.

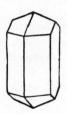 

Figure 106   Gypsum

Also found in Group VI is by far the largest family of minerals on the Earth — the *Silicates*. Although there is a vast range in composition which is frequently very complex, X-ray investigation has shown certain basic facts about atomic structure in the Silicate group, and their intricate compositions. The most fundamental structural unit of all Silicates is a silica tetrahedron with four oxygen

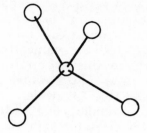

Figure 107   Silica tetrahedron

atoms surrounding each atom of silicon. But these SiO_2 groups may be linked together in various ways to form an indefinitely extended series. The basic Silicate tetrahedron is shown in Figure 107. We must remember that quartz, although composed of pure silica (SiO_2), is not included in this group because it is a simple oxide of the metal silicon.

The largest group of crystals in the bulk of the crust are the feldspars, which fall into two groups.

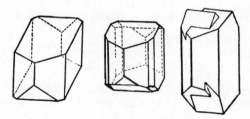

Figure 108   Orthoclase feldspar

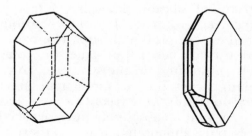

Figure 109   Albite feldspar

The first is made of various combinations of potassium and sodium in combination with aluminium and silica. The potassium and sodium can vary from zero to one hundred per cent, and the name that is given to any particular feldspar in this group is dependent on its potassium/sodium ratio. The two major sodium feldspars are orthoclase ($KA1Si_3O_8$), which crystallizes in the Monoclinic system, and microcline, with the same chemical formula but which crystallizes in the Triclinic system. These feldspars are generally pink in colour and are the minerals that give granite its characteristically pink hue. The other main group of feldspars is based on sodium and calcium, for the sodium and calcium vary in percentage just as the potassium and sodium did in the previous series. Crystals of these two groups of feldspars are shown in Figures 108 and 109.

I. *Aluminum Garnet,* including
    A. GROSSULARITE Calcium-Aluminum Garnet $Ca_3Al_2(SiO_4)_3$
    B. PYROPE   Magnesium-Aluminum Garnet $Mg_3Al_2(SiO_4)_3$
    C. ALMANDITE   Iron-Aluminum Garnet $Fe_3Al_2(SiO_4)_3$
    D. SPESSARTITE Manganese-Aluminum Garnet $Mn_3Al_2(SiO_4)_3$

II. *Iron Garnet,* including
    E. ANDRADITE   Calcium-Iron Garnet $Ca_3Fe_2(SiO_4)_3$
    (1) Ordinary. (2) Magnesian. (3) Titaniferous. (4) Yttriferous.

III. *Chromium Garnet.*
    F. UVAROVITE   Calcium-Chromium Garnet $Ca_3Cr_2(SiO_4)_3$

Another group of silicate minerals commonly encountered is the garnet group. Table 1 shows various types of garnet, and their chemical make-up. The basic structure of each group of garnets is the same, with one or more metals freely substituting in the structure. In the case of the aluminium garnet, the calcium, magnesium, iron and manganese tend to substitute freely with one another, and thus we seldom find an absolutely pure pyrope garnet or an absolutely pure almandite garnet, as there is always a certain amount of intermixing. Crystals of garnets are

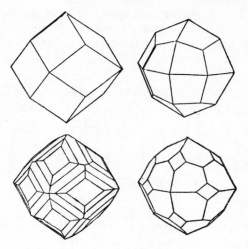

Figure 110   Garnet

shown in Figure 110. Although garnet is normally thought of as a red mineral, it may also be colourless, yellow, cinnamon brown, or emerald green (once again pointing out the difficulty of trying to classify minerals by colour). The name garnet is from the latin word *granitus*, meaning 'like a grain', and directly from *pomegranate*, the seeds of

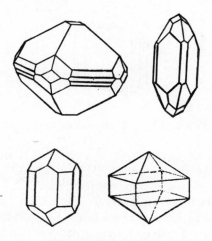

Figure 111   Zircon

which are small, numerous and red. The name almandite is probably derived from the ancient city of Alabanda, where the alabandic carbuncles of Pliny were cut and polished.

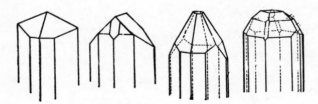

Figure 112   Topaz

The foregoing examples give two of the major mineral series within the Silicates, and we will now briefly list other silicate minerals that the reader is likely to encounter.

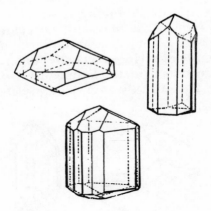

Figure 113   Tourmaline crystals

These include zircon ($ZrSiO_4$), crystals of which are shown in Figure 111; topaz ($Al(F,OH)_2 (AlSiO)_4$, crystals of which are shown in Figure 112; tourmaline ($H_9Al_3(B.OH)_2Si_4O_{19}$), crystals of which are shown in Figure 113; staurolite ($HFeAl_5Si_2O_{13}$), crystals of which are shown in Figure 114; sphene ($CaTiSiO_5$), and aquamarine (beryl)($Be_3Al_2(SiO_3)_6$, shown in Figure 115.

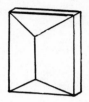
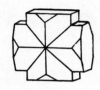

Figure 114   Staurolite crystals

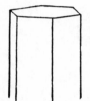
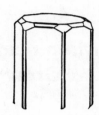
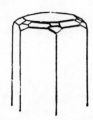

Figure 115   Beryl crystals

Another series of minerals within the silicates that might be encountered, although probably not in distinctive crystals, are the micas. The micas form very thin, flexible and transparent to semi-transparent sheets. As with the garnets and feldspars, the micas form a complete group of minerals within themselves, all of which contain aluminium and silica, and may also have various combinations of potassium, magnesium, sodium and lithium. They also all contain water within the crystal's structure. The common name by which several of the transparent species are known, is isinglass, which was often used as the transparent 'windows' in old wood-burning stoves.

Other silicate minerals often encountered that do not often form large single crystals are serpentine, talc and all of the various minerals such as kaolin that make up the clay minerals.

The last two groups, VII, *Salts of Organic Acids*, and Group VIII, *Hydrocarbon Compounds*, are not discussed since they do not form crystals of any size.

In this chapter, then, we have examined how crystals and minerals are studied and classified. In the next chapter, we will see how they form in the Earth.

4.

The Environments of Crystal Growth

We have seen how minerals and their crystals form from accumulations of atoms. In this chapter, as part of our study of the environments in which crystals form, we shall also look at accumulations of crystallized minerals which form major structural components of the Earth's crust. And therein, we have the scientific definition of the word *rock*. By definition, a rock is composed of one or more minerals, and is a major component of the crust. Although most rocks are mixtures of two or more minerals, if a single mineral exists on a large enough scale, it may also be considered a rock, mainly because it is an integral part of the structure of the Earth. A common example of a rock composed of only one mineral is limestone, composed of the mineral calcite. A rock familiar to most readers, granite, is a rock composed of at least three minerals: quartz, feldspar and mica. The actual name a rock is given in geology depends on its mineral content and the size of its crystals.

Rocks form in three basic environments: igneous, metamorphic and sedimentary. The environments in which these three different types of rocks form provides us with certain distinct growing environments for crystals.

Igneous rock is formed from molten rock, *sedimentary* rock through the deposition of wind and water, and *metamorphic* rock is formed through changes in other types of rock through heat and pressure that has not involved remelting.

Igneous Rock

The origin of igneous rock is deep in the Earth and it forms from a body of molten rock called a *magma*. Within the deep crust these magmas are probably not molten as we would think of the term, but exist in what is called by scientists a *plastic* state, having a consistency and strength similar to that of honey. Due to the shifting of the continents, zones of weakness and cracks occur in the overlying rocks and it is this release of pressure from the magma that allows the temperature to rise, and for them to become sufficiently molten to flow upward through these cracks.

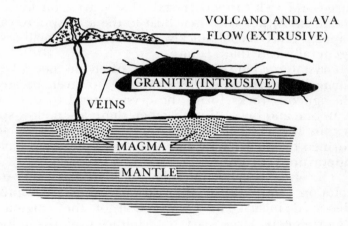

Figure 116   Extrusive and intrusive rocks

As the magma rises, it continues upwards through the crack and out onto the surface of the Earth as a volcano or as a lava flow. Such rocks are said to be extruded onto the surface and are called *extrusive* rocks. Or the magma may reach a point within another, much cooler, rock layer where it solidifies without reaching the surface. These types of igneous rock are known as *intrusive* rocks, because they have intruded or forced their way into other existing rocks (Figure 116). This process has been going on since the creation of the Earth and igneous rocks are being formed in the same way today as they have been during the long history of our planet. We know that there are numerous active volcanos throughout the world — certainly the most obvious types of igneous activity; but the action of intrusion, or the formation of intrusive rocks, is much slower, and being below the surface of the Earth, is quite invisible to us. Readers may be interested to realize that as they are reading this book, they may be sitting on top of intrusive rocks which are forming crystals at this very instant.

Since intrusive rocks cool much more slowly than extrusive rocks, due to the insulating effects of the rocks surrounding them, there is a great deal more time for crystals to form, and intrusive rocks generally are made of large and well-formed crystals. Extrusives, on the other hand, since they lose their heat to the atmosphere rather rapidly, tend to cool quickly, and form only small crystals (generally less than 1mm).

Crystals making up intrusives often do not take the forms illustrated in earlier chapters, however, because as the igneous rocks form, the crystals tend to inter-grow with one another. It is only when there are hollow spaces within the crystallizing intrusive rocks, such as those formed by gas bubbles, that well-formed crystals have an opportunity to grow.

The igneous magma may be considered as a very dense solution, with all of the various atomic constituents dissolved in it. The composition of the magma will determine in large part the character of the minerals which compose the resulting rocks. It is shown that the following constitute about 99 per cent of the elements present in the crust of the Earth: oxygen, silicon, aluminium, iron, magnesium, calcium, sodium and potassium, in that order. These elements occur in varying proportions in igneous rocks; the constituent minerals of igneous rocks are composed of them. The conditions under which the various minerals are formed are complex, but generally speaking, they crystallize from the cooling magma in the order of solubility. Although this order is fairly definite, the variations in chemical composition of the magma will affect the degree of solubility of the various mineral constituents, and thus the order of their crystallization can be altered. It is also known that the presence of small amounts of substances such as water vapour, carbon dioxide, fluorine gas and sulphur will greatly influence the temperatures at which various minerals crystallize. As all of these additional substances will be present in varying amounts, the crystallizing temperatures can vary considerably.

In fact, it has been shown that unless substances such as water vapour or carbon dioxide are present, crystals will not form at all. It has been demonstrated that minerals such as quartz and feldspar can rarely be formed from dry fusion — that is, without the presence of some of these extra gases. When this is attempted, uncrystallized glasses result. But, in the presence of only a fraction of a percentage of water vapour, excellent crystals will form. These additional substances are called mineralizers.

A type of igneous activity that concerns us even more than the formation of large rock-bodies are those crystals that form from the high temperature hot water solutions left over when magmas have crystallized. When the molten rock cools and solidifies, large quantities of liquid and gas charged with mineral matter are given off. Leaving the igneous rocks behind them, they make their way slowly toward the surface through cracks in the surrounding rock, forming mineral deposits wherever conditions are favourable. Thus, lower temperature, reduced pressure and the presence of limestone or other easily changed rocks are conducive to the deposition of certain types of crystals. As these mineral laden solutions flow into natural cracks in other rocks, crystals form. Such a filled-in fissure is called a *vein*. The solutions filling these veins often contain such metals as copper, lead, gold, silver and zinc, and it is from such veins that almost all of our precious metals originate, and many of the other economically important ones (Figure 116).

But there is one type of vein in particular that is of interest to us, as the crystals from such veins are usually well formed and often quite large. This type of vein is called a *pegmatite* and is characterized by its large crystals.

Single crystals from such veins have been recorded up to 40 feet in length, and crystals of a foot or more are not all that uncommon. Pegmatites are normally associated with the formation of granites, and the basic crystals that form in them are the major minerals of granite — quartz, feldspar and mica. All three minerals are often present in pegmatites, but it is not unusual to find one made up entirely of quartz, or feldspar.

In this type of vein, there is a flow of hot water solution (several hundred degrees centigrade and under great pressure) carrying the dissolved components of the various minerals; as the solution flows through the vein, the crystals form as linings, each crystal forming one layer of atoms at a time. In a typical pegmatite, the first crystals deposited will be feldspars, followed by a layer of quartz, and then by mica crystals.

Figure 117   A hypothetical pegmatite

The next stage of crystallization in a pegmatite depends on which metals are present in the solution. If the metal zirconium is present, then zircons form. If berillium is present, the mineral beryl forms (the blue variety of which is aquamarine, and the green variety, emerald). If fluorine is present, either the mineral fluorite may form or, under certain conditions, topaz; if boron is present, tourmaline may form. Or, if various combinations of calcium, magnesium, manganese or iron are present garnet may form. Quite clearly, such veins are of vital interest to the student of crystals. Figure 117 shows a hypothetical pegmatite.

In such veins, crystals always grow to fill the largest space available. If a crystal grows directly opposite another crystal where their points would meet if they grew toward each other, both will grow diagonally to miss each other. Usually a crystal will grow into the largest open space available to it, even if has to grow at a considerable angle to the vein wall. Some such crystals will grow almost sideways. This presumably reflects the desire of the *elemental* of the crystal to grow as large a crystal as possible in the space available — thus perpetuating that type of crystal to the largest extent. More about elementals will be discussed in the Energies chapter.

Certain crystals also grow from vapour, such crystals being mainly confined to volcanic regions, where mineralized gases are escaping through vents. Minerals deposited in this way are sulphur, realgar and hematite.

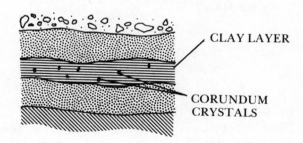

CLAY LAYER

CORUNDUM CRYSTALS

Figure 118

Metamorphic Rocks

Metamorphic rocks are formed from either igneous, sedimentary, or even other metamorphic rocks, and are rocks which have undergone some sort of physical or chemical change after their original formation. This change has normally been brought about by high temperatures and pressures, aided by the action of water vapour and other chemical agents. These changes often involve the adding or subtracting of constituents to or from the existing minerals, and often involve the formation of new minerals that are more stable under the new conditions. Although many of the original minerals may continue to exist, there are others that are characteristically developed during the process of metamorphism. Such characteristic minerals are kyanite, staurolite, talc and grossularite garnet (a green garnet). Figure 118 shows how such a process can take place. In this instance, a layer of alumina-rich clay is formed in a shallow inland sea. It has been covered over by a layer of sand, and eventually by layer upon layer of sand and gravel, as the area in which the lake existed gradually sank due to deformation of the Earth's crust. Eventually the pressure and temperature due to the deep burial rose to the point where the alumina began to recrystallize, to form hexagonal crystals of the mineral corundum (sapphire and ruby).

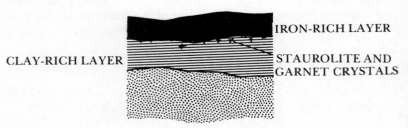

CLAY-RICH LAYER

IRON-RICH LAYER

STAUROLITE AND GARNET CRYSTALS

Figure 119

In Figure 119 this same alumina-rich layer has had another clay layer deposited on top of it, but this time the overlying clay was rich in iron oxide. During a similar deformation of the crust, as in Figure 118, temperatures and pressures were high enough this time to allow the atoms of iron to become highly mobile, as were the atoms of alumina. As silicas were also available from the clay, all of these available atoms rearranged themselves to form the mineral staurolite ($HFeAl_5Si_2O_{13}$).

There are several minerals which occur in metamorphic

rocks that also occur in igneous rocks, such as garnet, spinel and corundum. It can be seen that where igneous and metamorphic rocks are concerned, the basic chemical processes take place at a high temperature and pressure, and in many instances the dividing line between them is rather thin.

There is another type of metamorphic environment called contact metamorphism. This occurs when an igneous body has been intruded into a surrounding rock, causing heating and remelting of the surrounding rock, and where gases of the igneous body have escaped into the surrounding rocks. If the metamorphosed rock happens to be limestone, there are a number of minerals which can form due to the recrystallization of the limestone in combination with mineral constituents of the intruding materials. Garnets can form, along with spinel, corundum and pyroxene. Contact metamorphic deposits can also produce tourmaline, topaz and fluorite, although not commonly.

Sedimentary Rock
This type of rock is formed through the processes of wind and water. Crystals which form in these types of rocks are almost always formed from low temperature water solutions and are usually quite soft (because of the low energies involved in bonding the atoms together). These crystals appear to form quite rapidly, and in some places where crystals are regularly dug out of deposits such as quicksand, further crystals seem to form within about a year. Crystals found in quicksands are the so-called 'Desert Roses', which are multiple crystals of the mineral selenite (crystalline gypsum). Another common sedimentary mineral found in extensive deposits is halite (rock salt), often found in deposits hundreds of feet thick. But by far the most common mineral formed in sedimentary environments is the mineral calcite, which forms the rock limestone. Another commercially important sedimentary mineral is barite (bayrtes), which forms beautiful blue crystals somewhat resembling aquamarine.

How long does it actually take for most crystals to form? For the most part, we simply do not know. In the laboratory, quartz crystals several inches in length can be grown in a matter of weeks, and it is possible that in nature, such crystals may form almost as rapidly.

To grow a transparent crystal of several inches requires constant growing conditions — few changes in temperature or pressure. In a natural environment stable conditions over a long period (say a year) are most unlikely, thus we would expect most crystals to form over a much shorter period. Certainly not the millions of years commonly thought.

5.

From Earth to Hand

In this chapter we shall explore further how crystals are found, mined, and how they make their way to the user. There are two major types of crystal deposit — veins, which we have discussed previously, and the *placer* deposit. The placer is a water or wind-layed deposit, composed of the fragments of decomposed veins. Certain types of crystals, particularly those that are harder and more resistant to weathering, such as diamond, sapphire, ruby, zircon and topaz, also happen to be heavier than the vein minerals in which they form and often concentrate in beach and stream deposits. Virtually all of the sapphires and rubies and at least half of the diamonds produced in the world come from such deposits. Placer deposits containing crystals are often discovered by accident, or through the mining of other minerals, such as gold.

There are a number of techniques used for the mining and extraction of crystals.

Diamond is a crystal that can be recovered by actually mining and crushing the rock in which it grows, but most crystals are too fragile for this process. Once the diamond-bearing rock has been crushed, it is then mixed with water, and floated across special grease-coated tables. Since water does not stick to the diamonds, which remain perfectly dry, they stick to the grease. The other stone, being wet, does not stick and washes away. The grease bearing the diamonds is then scraped off, boiled away, and nothing but diamond remains. The diamonds are then graded and sorted, and the gem quality stones are sent to the various gem cutting centres of the world, the most important of which are Amsterdam and Tel Aviv.

Crystals which grow in veins or in pegmatites, are often mined by native miners using tools as simple as a hammer and chisel. More complex mining operations, using rock drills, explosives and bulldozers, are also used in areas which produce sufficient quality and quantity of crystals to make such expensive methods worthwhile. Sometimes it is necessary to follow a vein for many feet before it will open up into a hollow where crystals are able to form perfectly. Such openings are called *vugs* and may contain hundreds of pounds of crystals and be many feet across. These are typical of mining in pegmatite areas.

The working of placer deposits is another type of mining altogether. The crystals that are mined from placers, such as sapphire, ruby, zircon, garnet, and topaz, are significantly heavier than the gravels in which they occur, and when they are washed in water tend to concentrate at the bottom of the container. A common method of mining in such deposits is to sieve the crystal-bearing gravels; by shaking the sieves under water in a certain pattern, the heavier constituents of the gravel can be easily concentrated at a particular place on the bottom of the sieve. The sieves are then turned over without disturbing the gravel, and the crystals that are of interest can simply be picked off. This method is commonly used by small scale mining operations, such as those operated by one or two men. Surprisingly, with the exception of diamond and emerald, the majority of the gem materials available on the market has come from thousands of one or two man operations.

In larger scale placer mines, crystal-bearing gravels are run through *sluices*, which are nothing more than open troughs through which a stream of water is flowing. Cleats are placed at the bottom of the troughs across the flow of water in order to keep the heavy minerals, which drop to the bottom, from being washed out. Gravel is then shovelled into the boxes, and the flow of water mechanically separates the heavier minerals and washes out the light ones. At the end of the day the box is emptied and all of the heavy crystals will be caught in the cleats at the bottom of the box. In areas where particularly valuable stones are found these sluices may be dozens of feet in length. This is also a common method of washing for gold.

After the miners have collected their crystals, through whichever method, they are often sold to travelling buyers who move from one small mine to the next. In some countries, such as Columbia, crystal output is controlled by the government, and the buyers are often government agents. The various batches of crystals are then taken to whichever city serves as the exporting centre for the country involved, where international buyers come to make their selections. Crystals are then shipped by the most convenient means possible. If the importer is buying uncut gemstones, he may well carry his purchase away in a briefcase or a coat pocket. If the buyer has purchased large crystals, such as Brazilian quartz or amethyst crystals, they are frequently shipped in steel drums weighing several hundred pounds each. It is not unusual for an importer to buy 50 to 100 of these drums at any one time. The importer then redistributes the crystals he has purchased to various mineral dealers.

Thus the crystal which you purchase may have begun its travels by being washed from a stream or dug from a hillside by a native prospector thousands of miles away, and began its journey to you in a knapsack, or on the back of a burro.

Let us now examine where and how crystals of various minerals are found.

Diamond Of all crystals produced by the Earth, there is probably more mythology surrounding diamond than any other. The earliest diamonds to appear in the gem market came from India, and it is speculated that diamonds were discovered as long as 5000 years ago. There was no real interest in diamonds until medieval times, however, and it was not until well into the sixteenth century that the diamond mines in India began to be worked in earnest. These were all placer deposits, as were the deposits in

Brazil that were discovered late in the eighteenth century. The Indian mines have long been worked out, but they have produced some remarkable stones, including the Kohi-Nor, (meaning 'Mountain of Light'), which weighed about 800 carats (there are 5 carats in a gram) when it was discovered.

The Brazilian mines were the main producers of diamonds until the discovery of deposits in South Africa in 1850. The first discoveries in South Africa were also in placer deposits, and in the decomposed parent rock of the volcanic pipes from which they are now mined. Amazingly, when the harder, un-decomposed level was reached in the Kimberley mines, the original miners began to abandon their claims, thinking there was no reason for digging further down — now some of these mines have reached a depth of a mile or more.

Although diamonds are found in volcanic pipes, the type of volcano which produces diamonds would probably be quite unrecognizable as such. Diamonds appear to originate in the mantle and are brought to the surface already crystallized. The flow of materials upward takes place in a relatively cool state, probably no more than a few hundred degrees centigrade, shown by the fact that there is little alteration of the surrounding rocks. It appears that the diamond-bearing rock simply flows to the surface as a 'slush' of already crystallized material. It is possible that diamond may be a fairly common constituent of the mantle. Small diamonds are also commonly found in nickle-iron meteorites, although not in economic quantity.

Diamonds have also been found in the USA and Guyana in South America, but the largest producer outside of Africa is the Soviet Union, although recent discoveries in Australia may make it the largest single producing country. Most diamonds are controlled by the De Beers Syndicate, and price levels are artificially maintained.

Ruby and Sapphire Ruby and sapphire are both varieties of the same mineral, corundum. Their properties are identical, differing only in colour. They are both made of aluminium oxide, but ruby contains traces of chromium, and sapphire traces of titanium. Sapphire can also occur in green, purple, yellow and pink. Each of these colours is caused by minute traces of other elements in the crystal structure. For many centuries there was no effort to distinguish genuine rubies from other red stones, and many red stones were called rubies even though mineralogically they bore no resemblance. Two of the world's most famous 'rubies', the Black Prince's Ruby and the Timur, both in the British Crown Jewels, are not rubies at all, but are red varieties of spinel.

Sapphire is also another name that appears in ancient literature, but once again it referred to other blue stones and not to what we know today as sapphire. Most 'sapphire' in ancient writings was probably lapis lazuli.

The richest sources of sapphire were stream gravels in Sri Lanka, which produced literally tons of sapphire and small amounts of ruby over the centuries. Thailand and Burma have also produced quantities of sapphire and small amounts of ruby. Modern supplies now also come from Australia, Brazil and the state of Montana in the USA. All of these mines are placer deposits.

Good quality ruby is now the most valuable gemstone, being more valuable even than diamonds, emeralds, or sapphires of the equivalent size. Large rubies are rare, because chromium, the colouring agent of ruby, has a strongly inhibiting effect on crystal growth.

Emerald and Aquamarine Emerald and aquamarine are both varieties of the mineral beryl, a silicate of beryllium. The green coloration of emerald is due to minute traces of chromium, and of aquamarine from minute traces of iron. Emerald and aquamarine have different growing environments and are not usually found together. Aquamarine almost always occurs in pegmatites; emeralds in contact metamorphics, often associated with altered slates. The largest supplies of aquamarine come from the pegmatites of Brazil and from placer deposits in Sri Lanka. The chief source of emerald is from Columbia and Brazil. The largest known emerald weighs 1,350 carats and is nearly a foot in length. Other crystals of the mineral beryl which have a use as gemstones are the yellow variety called heliodor; morganite, which is pink, and goshenite — a colourless variety. Crystals of beryl up to 40 feet in length have been found.

Tourmaline Tourmaline is another mineral commonly found in pegmatite deposits and is usually mined directly from the vein, although it is quite resistant to weathering and is also found in placer deposits. Tourmaline comes in a number of colours but the most common is green, varying from an olive green to a very dark and almost opaque green. It also occurs in red, orange and blue. Brazil, Sri Lanka, Madagascar, and South Africa are the most important sources. It usually occurs in well developed and perfectly formed crystals.

Garnet The term garnet applies to a whole group of minerals having a varied chemical composition but a similar internal structure. Garnets are usually thought of as red, but they are also common in green, brown or black. Single garnet crystals the size of grapefruits have been found, and crystals the size of hen's eggs are not at all uncommon.

Garnets occur most commonly in metamorphic rocks, but they are also found in certain types of igneous rocks such as pegmatites and in certain deep-seated types of magmas, such as those in which diamonds are found.

Gem quality garnet is found in a wide variety of places throughout the world, where it is usually recovered from placer deposits, most often as a result of the mining of other more precious minerals. Virtually any area where metamorphic rocks are found will produce garnets in some profusion, although they may not be of collectable quality.

Quartz In the previous chapter we have discussed the numerous varieties of quartz and it will be hard to find a place on the Earth where one or more varieties are not present. We shall look only at the crystal varieties, since they are of the most direct interest to us.

Rock crystal, the colourless variety, often forms very perfect crystals and is found in virtually every area of the world where igneous activity has occurred. It is commonly mined direct from the vein, where it may be recovered in huge crystals. In the USA, in the State of Arkansas, quartz pegmatites have been intruded through sandstones in almost vertical sheets. The sandstone, which is quite crumbly, is dug away with bulldozers, leaving the sheets of crystal to fall apart, often revealing thousands of crystals up to a foot or more in length on a single sheet. In Brazil, rock crystal is also mined directly from the pegmatite, and is also recovered from the clay-based soils into which weathered pegmatites have deposited their crystal. Most of the rock crystal available on the world market comes from these two sources, although there are thousands of minor sources.

Amethyst, the purple variety of quartz, also occurs in excellent crystals and is found in a number of places throughout the world. Uruguay and Brazil are major producers of high quality material and, to a lesser extent, Australia. Amethyst is usually mined directly from the vein and it is also frequently found in large crystal lined cavities which form in the hollow spaces left by gas bubbles in solidified lavas. Once again, there are hundreds of minor sources of amethyst worldwide.

Citrine and smoky quartz are also found in a number of places and are also often mined directly from the pegmatite, or from decomposed pegmatites. Normally pegmatites bearing either of these minerals are found intruded through granitic rocks, which often carry with them a certain amount of naturally radioactive material, providing the gamma radiation that causes the coloration. Naturally occurring citrine and smoky quartz comes principally from Brazil, although once again there are a number of lesser sources. Much of the material available on the market has been artifically coloured by subjecting colourless crystals to radiation.

Topaz Topaz usually occurs in pegmatite deposits where fluorine gas has been present. It is dense and hard, and is frequently found in placer deposits. It is also found during normal mining activities in pegmatite type deposits.

It is commonly thought of as being yellow in colour, but it is more commonly found either as colourless crystals or in blue, pink, and light green. Crystals of topaz can be quite large, and well formed crystals a foot or more in length and weighing several hundred pounds are occasionally found.

The pegmatite deposits of Brazil and Mexico currently produce most of the world's supply of topaz, although splendid gem quality crystals are coming into the market now from Siberia. There are also significant deposits of topaz in the USA, Africa and Tasmania.

Zircon Zircon is a fairly common constituent of granite, although it does not always form crystals large enough to be visible. It is found in larger crystals in a number of places in the world, normally where it has concentrated in placer deposits. Crystals of good form and gem quality are found mainly in the deposits of Sri Lanka and Thailand, but also in Canada, Madagascar and the USA. Generally speaking, zircon crystals seldom exceed two inches in length.

Zircon comes in a number of colours including blue, yellow, orange, green and in colourless stones which resemble diamonds.

In the previous listings we have discussed many crystals that are also used as gemstones. There are other gem, materials, whose names are familiar to the reader, that we have not mentioned, because either they do not form crystals, or because the crystals are so difficult to obtain that the reader would be unlikely ever to encounter them (such as Chrysoberyl). Those which do not commonly form distinct crystals are amber, jade, turquoise, lapis lazuli.

In the following portion of this chapter we will discuss other minerals that form crystals that are readily available, but that are not considered as gemstones.

Pyrite Pyrite is the mineral known in the days of the Wild West as 'fool's gold', as its colour and lustre were easily mistaken for gold when it appeared in the pans of early prospectors. It is composed totally of iron and sulphur and is mined extensively in a number of areas in the world for use in the manufacture of sulphuric acid, and as a minor ore of iron. It forms excellent and distinct crystals, which can be up to several inches across. It is found in every area of the world where ore deposits have been found and is mined directly from the vein. It is also found in small amounts in coal and slate, often as well formed crystals.

Fluorite Fluorite is composed of calcium and fluorine and is mined in a number of areas throughout the world for use as a flux in the manufacture of steel. It usually forms cubic crystals, but the fluorite specimens commonly available on the market are octahedral in shape and are formed by cleaving fragments of large crystals. Its colour can range from lemon yellow to rich purple, and it can also be green, pink and colourless. Most of the collectors' specimens on the market come from the USA, although splendid crystals have been found in the past in the Swiss Alps.

Calcite Crystallized calcite is formed in water deposited veins, usually in sedimentary rocks. It forms magnificent crystals, often several inches in length. The perfectly transparent variety, usually cleaved into rhombohedrons, is called Iceland Spar. This is used in several sorts of optical devices, due to its peculiar light transmitting properties. The largest commercial deposits of calcite are found in Mexico, although it is a common constituent of sedimentary rocks worldwide.

Apatite The name apatite comes from a Greek word meaning 'to deceive', because of its resemblance to other minerals. Well formed, yellow crystals come from Mexico, and it is also found in purple and green crystals. The largest deposits are situated in the Soviet Union, where it is mined for fertilizer on account of its high phosphate content.

Feldspar As previously discussed, the feldspar group is the single largest rock-forming mineral group on the Earth in terms of total bulk. Well formed crystals of its various varieties are available and there are certain varieties that find use as gemstones. The most commonly known variety is moonstone, which appears to be a microscopic intergrowth of orthoclase and albite. Other gem varieties are labradorite, which shows iridescent colours when polished, and amazonstone, a green variety of orthoclase. Well-crystallized varieties of feldspars are usually mined directly from pegmatites, or recovered from the soils of decomposed pegmatites.

Aragonite Aragonite is of the same chemical composition as calcite but has crystallized in a different structure. Large well-formed crystals are commonly available and are usually twin crystals. Mother-of-Pearl, Oyster, and Abalone shells are all made of aragonite. Aragonite is found in many countries, but the best crystals come from Spain.

Staurolite Staurolite is a common constituent of metamorphic rocks, but it does not necessarily form good crystals. However, in a few places in the world it forms interesting twin crystals, forming either equal-arm crosses or St Andrew's crosses. The major source for staurolite is in the USA, but they are also found in Switzerland and Australia.

6.

Minerals Through the Ages

The history of man and the history of man's use of minerals are intertwined. It is only within the last 3000 years, a mere instant in time compared with the several million years that man has been making tools, that metal has replaced stone as the primary tool-making material. The most recent archaeological discoveries indicate that man's ancestors were using stone for tool making well over three million years ago. The time in which man discovered and actually began to use crystals is unknown, but Jeffrey Goodman, in his book *Psychic Archaeology*, speculates that men may have been collecting crystals for healing purposes as much as 100,000 years ago in North America.

Crystals were the most powerful single objects in use during the period of Atlantis. They were the principal source of energy and their powers were unsurpassed in healing. But, as with all tools of man, these powers and energies were also subject to misuse and it was the misuse of these very powers that caused the downfall of the Atlantean civilization. It was also at this time that many of the energies that focused through crystals were withdrawn from the Earth. It is only now, when the Earth has finally begun to recover from the trauma of Atlantis, that these powers and energies are once again being returned to mankind. This is the reason behind the impulse being felt by so many people worldwide to study and learn more about crystals.

The approaching end of Atlantis was known in advance by the uncorrupted members of the priesthood, and there was a great outflowing from Atlantis of priests carrying the Ancient Knowledge to all of the other less developed civilizations of the Earth. It was known that if these seeds of knowledge were planted in as many places as possible, it was inevitable that certain of them would survive and flower, and new spiritual civilizations would spring up on the Earth. These were the roots such civilizations as the Tibetan and the Egyptian.

By about 3000 BC the Egyptian priesthood felt sufficiently confident in their spiritual progress to attempt to recreate certain aspects of the Atlantean civilization. It was at this time that the Great Pyramid was built, being modelled on the Golden Temple of Atlantis. The capstone of the Great Pyramid, a crystal, was once again able to draw in small measure on certain of the powers and energies that had not been fully withdrawn after Atlantis. Once again, however, the priesthood became corrupted, and those powers remaining were totally withdrawn.

The use of particular stones later in Egypt, although not necessarily crystals, became important through their use in the construction of amulets. Other materials, such as bone, shell and metals of various kinds, were also used for this purpose, but it is not known exactly what properties, if any, were ascribed to stone amulets. The materials commonly used were cryptocrystalline, such as carnelian, agate, turquoise and lapis lazuli.

Through this same time period, the Babylonians and Assyrians were using various stones and crystals for amulets. The most important class of these were cylinder seals, made of a number of different types of stone. An Assyrian text which has survived says that seals made of Ka-Gi-Ma stone will help a man to destroy his enemy. A seal made of lapis lazuli contains a god, and 'His God will rejoice in him'. It was also said that a seal made of rock crystal will extend the possessions of a man and a seal made from green serpentine will draw many blessings to it. The possessor of a seal made from red jasper or carnelian will never be separated from the protection of his God. Even at that time a popular mythology had begun to grow up around the use of particular stones.

Also within this same time period is probably the best known example of the use of stones for magical purposes — an object known to history as the Breast Plate of Aaron. Because much of the mythology concerning this object is covered in other texts, an actual description is unnecessary but a few comments are relevant on certain of the stones that are listed. Stones said to have been in the Breast Plate emphasize one of the greatest single problems that the modern scholar has in dealing with old texts and descriptions, which is that certain mineral names have been applied through history to a variety of different substances, most of which are entirely unrelated to the present substance called by that name. For example, in ancient times the term 'sapphire' was frequently applied to any blue stone, and in the Breast Plate itself may have referred to lapis-lazuli. In many translations diamond is listed as one of the principal stones of the Plate; however, it must be remembered that in the biblical description of the Breast Plate, the name of one of the twelve tribes of Israel was engraved on the corresponding stone of the Breast Plate. With the technology available at that time it is utterly impossible to have ground a flat face on a diamond, much less to have engraved on it. Another stone listed in the Breast Plate is carbuncle. A number of different writers guess at what this stone might have been but although the evidence points to almandine garnet, there is no great certainty on this point. Thus, we see the problem of old texts and legends, in that we are never certain that the stone referred to is one that is known today by that name.

The first serious writing regarding stones does not appear until about 300 BC, when Theophrastus, a student of Aristotle, wrote a thesis entitled *On Stones*. The work comprises 120 short paragraphs and in them he describes what a modern mineralogist would recognize as about sixteen mineral species. Most of the remainder is involved in the description of the then known metals and certain 'earths' (ochre, marls, clay, etc.).

The next ancient author of note was the Roman author Pliny, who lived between AD 23 and 79. He was killed observing the eruption of Mount Vesuvius that buried

Pompeii. His writings, entitled *Natural History*, were probably called an Encyclopaedia, and comprised 37 books. Only portions of the last four books relate to stones, however. This is the most voluminous of ancient works on the subject. To give some idea of the small quantity of ancient writings available, the whole of his writings on minerals and crystals would comprise no more than perhaps fifteen pages of this text.

It must be remembered that both Theophrastus and Pliny were simply compilers of information: they neither worked with, nor in all probability could even identify, all of the stones that they describe.

Most of what is written from the time of Pliny until the reawakening of learning in the early sixteenth century was more related to alchemy than directly to the study of minerology. Alchemy, at least in the purely scientific sense of the term, relates more to metallurgy than to mineralogy, but there are nonetheless occasional references to minerals in the writings of several authors.

We owe much of the preservation of early writings such as that of Aristotle and Pliny to the Arabs, who preserved scientific knowledge at a time when Europe had sunk into the Dark Ages, when much of the work of earlier writers disappeared into the chaos.

One of the Arabs to whom we owe a great deal is Avicenna (980–1073) who was a physician of great note, and translated many of the Greek and Roman classics into Arabic. The next writer of importance during this period was Albertus Magnus, a Dominican monk, who was writing around 1270. Once again, though, it must be remembered that he was a compiler of other people's work. His writing on mineralogy, except for a few books on gems, is the only writing of any consequence on that subject between Pliny and Agricola.

It was during this period that much of the lore associated with the use of crystals and gems was accumulated. But it must be re-emphasized that the names applied to minerals in those days were not necessarily the same as those used today; many modern writers still fail to sort out modern from ancient terminology. Thus, in a book published as late as 1973, a writer can still list six different types of 'rubies', only one of which is actually ruby — the other five refer to different minerals altogether. What is even more extraordinary, is that in a book published in 1977, which has already gone through a second printing, is a list of names of 115 stones and their properties — of these, 97 are names totally unknown to modern mineralogy. It would be interesting to have the author of this book produce samples of the various minerals he lists!

Most early references to the various powers of stones seem to be related more to their colour than to anything else. The use of colour for healing is certainly a well-proven technique, and there is no doubt that the application of coloured stones would have much the same effect as the application of colour through any other medium. But this completely ignores the most valuable properties of crystals: their ability to transform energy, discussed in a later chapter.

The foregoing does not mean to imply that the users of crystals and minerals in the early literature were using them improperly or using them through ignorance. It is probable that some of these earlier users were working through their own intuitive powers, particularly at a time before intuition was less hampered by rationalism. But every claim made for a mineral must be given the most thorough testing through the use of open-minded intuition. We must likewise keep in mind that the energy of the Earth has changed dramatically since those effects were first observed, and since crystals respond to energy, we might expect a different response. Not only that, but as the Earth encompasses more and more Aquarian energy, we will see (through the intuition) changing reactions for our various crystals, requiring us to continually re-learn (or at least re-sensitize ourselves) to their energy responses.

We have examined some of the historical background of the science of mineralogy, in which the writers have done little more than accumulate bits and pieces of information from numerous sources. The modern science of mineralogy had to wait until 1546 for its real roots.

In this year, Georgius Agricola published his *De Natura Fossilium*, in which he classified minerals on the basis of

physical properties, actually studied and described minerals himself, and added new mineral descriptions to those
already published by earlier writers. In 1556 Agricola
published an even more remarkable book concerning
mining, mineralogy and metallurgy, called *De Re Metallica*.
This was the standard reference book for the mining
industry for over 200 years, and even today is one of the
most highly respected classics of scientific literature.

Following the lead of Agricola, others, such as Linneus
and Berzelius, began to study and classify minerals,
following the separate routes of classification by external
characteristics and by chemical composition.

But the true nature of minerals and crystals was waiting
for another science — chemistry — in order to provide a
basis and an explanation for many of the characteristics of
minerals. The concept of the atom had been around since
before Aristotle's day, but it fell to John Dalton, an English
chemist, to make the first step. Using the newly invented
burning glass, he heated the mineral cinnabar, an oxide of
mercury, in a closed container. He discovered that a very
pure gas was given off, which another chemist, A.L.
Lavosier, named oxygen. Although the concept of
chemical elements had been stated as early as 1661, this
was the first 'new' element to be discovered.

With the growth of modern atomic theory, the science
of mineralogy then had a first grounding for growth. By
1800, reliable chemical analysis of minerals began, and the
invention of the reflecting goniometer in 1809 made the
rapid and precise measurement of crystal angles possible.
By that time it was becoming apparent that chemical
composition and crystallographic characteristics were the
fundamental properties of minerals.

As more and more data became available, it fell to an
American, James White Dana, in 1837 to propose a system
of mineralogy based both on chemical constituents and
crystal structure, as discussed previously.

By the turn of the century the first experiments with
growing crystals synthetically were begun. The first crystal
grown in commercially viable amounts was sapphire,
produced in considerable quantities prior to the Second
World War. By that time, the use of this synthetic mineral

had almost entirely supplanted the use of natural sapphire for precision bearings in watches and meters.

The growth of the electronics industry in the 1950s and 1960s has also encouraged the production of synthetic quartz crystals, which have numerous electronic applications. By the 1970s, diamonds were being successfully synthesized on a commercial basis and dozens of minerals were being artifically grown in a variety of laboratory environments. It also became possible during this time to grow crystals that did not occur in nature, some of which have made possible remarkable advances in the electronics industry.

It is through these processes that our understanding of the hows and whys of crystal growth has progressed. In our understanding of how crystals grow in the laboratory, our understanding of natural processes has increased.

But will artifically grown crystals replace natural crystals as a contact point between Spirit and Matter? As we examine the various uses of crystals in the following chapter, we shall see.

7.

Crystal Energies

Before we discuss the behaviour of energies in crystals, it is useful to divide energies into two different groups.

The first group we will call *mundane energies*, defined as those energies that can be measured by current scientific methods — energies such as electricity, light, heat, and mechanical energy. The second group we will call *spiritual energies*, defined simply as energies that cannot be measured by current methods — such as the energies of thought, will, healing, and the energies that make up the higher spiritual bodies. We make this division, artificial though it may be, for a very important reason: we can describe quite precisely the behaviour of mundane energies within crystals, and from these descriptions we see that there are certain parallels with the behaviour of spiritual energies in crystals.

We begin by remembering our discussion of bonding in Chapter 2, and that the forces which tie a crystal together are in perfect balance and harmony. A crystal is in a perfect state of equilibrium — that is, apparently neither giving off energy nor taking it in. The evidence for this is quite simple — if it were taking in energy, it would be growing; if it were giving off energy, it would be shrinking. As it turns out, crystals are taking in and giving off energy constantly, but they are doing so in *perfect balance*. That is, the amount of energy given off is exactly equal to the amount of energy taken in, and thus the crystal remains unchanged. (There is one group of crystals where this is not true — the crystals of radioactive elements. In this case, energy is being given off all the time, but the crystal *does change*.) We will now look at some crystal examples, and see exactly how they maintain this perfect energy balance.

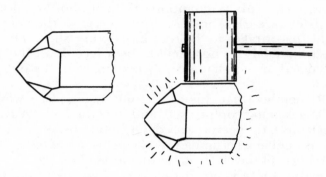

(a) UNSTRESSED CRYSTAL   (b) STRESSED CRYSTAL

Figure 120

The first behaviour we will examine is that of the *piezoelectric* effect (pronounced pie-ease-oh-electric). A crystal of quartz easily demonstrates this effect. In Figure 120a we see an ordinary quartz crystal with an 'A' axis pointing up, the atoms of its structure at a fixed distance from one another, all in perfect energy balance. In Figure 120b we strike the crystal with a mallet in the direction of the 'A' axis, compressing the structure momentarily. What we observe is a flash of visible light. What we do not see, unless we have special sensors, is that the crystal has also given off a burst of electricity. This effect of giving off visible light was well known to ancient man: quartz crystals are often found in American-Indian camp sites, and usually well battered.

In modern science, we do not simply strike the crystal with a mallet: we prepare precisely-made slices of crystal to compress mechanically; each slice is also connected to electronic measuring devices. In compressing the structure (and we are talking about a compression so small as to be almost unmeasurable), we are pushing the atoms slightly closer together and freeing the outer energy shell electrons from their necessity to bond quite so tightly. As we do this, electrons are freed from the outermost shell and move to the surface of the crystal. We remember from Chapter 2 that this transfer of electrons from one shell to another or, in this case, out of the shell entirely, is also connected with a quantum of light. So, we not only transfer free electrons, but we also release the amount of light that it takes to 'hold' it in its outer shell. The inner electron shells do not seem to be affected: all the effects discussed in this chapter only take place in the outermost shell.

Remember that this effect only takes place while the crystal is being compressed, and only until all the available electrons have been released. Once the compression stops, if it is held at a certain level (like being squeezed in a vice), and once all the electrons at that level of energy have been released, there is no further discharge. As in the case of our mallet, once the pressure is released, the crystal springs back to its original dimensions, and replaces its lost electrons by either drawing them back from the surface of the crystal, or by drawing free electrons from the air (where there are plenty of them). The crystal also re-absorbs enough light to 'glue' the electrons back into their proper shell positions. Even in a dark room, there is sufficient light energy available to do this, even though there is not enough to register on the human eye.

It is also possible to reverse this process. Rather than compress the crystal to give off electricity, we can put electricity (a flow of electrons) into the crystal to cause momentary expansion of the structure. What happens is that the influx of electrons momentarily overloads the outer shell, and the atoms drift slightly apart; but the electrons in these new positions are not stable and almost instantly break away to move on to the next plane of atoms. As they do so, the atoms that have been forced to part snap back into their original positions, until the next set of electrons comes along to repeat the cycle all over again. This alternating expansion and contraction of the crystal structure, then, is nothing more than vibration. If you had very sensitive fingers, you could feel the crystal vibrate physically. Or, if we put enough high energy electrons (higher amperage) into the crystal structure, we could actually blow it apart, but this is obviously not an experiment that many of us would be very happy to perform.

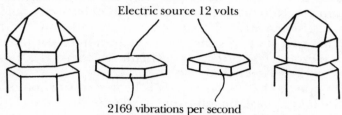

Electric source 12 volts

2169 vibrations per second

Figure 121   Quartz plates of identical dimensions from two different crystals

This ability of the crystal to vibrate has some other interesting twists — for example, if plates of the same thickness are cut from two or more different crystals (Figure 121) and the same amount of electrical energy is applied to each, the rate of vibration is exactly the same for each plate. This rate of vibration (called its frequency of vibration, because it is measured in vibrations per second) is a property that is widely employed in technology, particularly in quartz resonators for frequency control, in crystal pick-ups for gramophones, and in pressure gauges. Many readers will remember the old crystal radio sets, the crystal of which was nothing more than a slice of quartz crystal. In the earliest two-way radio sets, unless both sets had crystals of the same thickness (frequency) they were unable to 'talk' to one another.

It is this same property that many of you will be making use of even as you read this book — in the workings of your electronic watch. In this case, the quartz crystal in the watch is vibrating at a certain number of times per second. A small computer in the watch counts up the number of vibrations, and when it has counted up enough to equal a second, the second indicator advances by one. When this has happened sixty times, the minute indicator advances by one, and so forth.

The next effect is that of the application of heat to crystals, the result of which is known as *pyroelectricity*. It has been known for centuries in India and Ceylon that tourmaline, when heated in the embers of a fire, first attracted ashes and then repelled them. This phenomenon is due to electrical charges accumulating on the surface and occurs in the same crystals that show piezoelectricity. It appears to be closely related to piezoelectricity, in that crystals, when heated and cooled, expand and contract and are in a state of strain. The separation of pyroelectric and piezoelectric effects is difficult, as there is a rather close link between the two.

It appears that as the crystal is heated, distortion of the lattice takes place, possibly due to the number of electrons moving into higher energy shells as a result of the increased heat energy in the crystal. As in piezoelectricity, certain electrons are elevated enough in energy to break loose from the outer electron shells, and once again float to the surface of the crystal. In quartz, if the temperature is raised sufficiently, an entire new inner structure forms, called beta-quartz, but once the crystal cools it reverts to its original state, called alpha-quartz.

There is an easy demonstration of this electrical property, once again by heating tourmaline. A clean, dry crystal of tourmaline is heated to about 200° centigrade and then passed a few times through the flame of an alcohol lamp to dissipate the surface charges; it is then placed on a glass plate to cool. As it does so, a mixture of powdered red lead and sulphur is sifted over the crystal. The red lead goes to the negatively charged surfaces, and the sulphur to the positive areas. Again it is emphasized that as the crystal completely cools, it will re-absorb electrons into their proper structural position, and the crystal will go back to its original dimensions.

The next energy phenomenon is that of colour. Colour in a mineral in most instances is due to the absorption of certain wavelengths of light energy by the atoms making up the crystal. The wavelengths of white light that are not absorbed give the sensation of colour to the eye. Once again, it is the outer electrons that are involved; those of the deeper levels of the atom do not seem to be affected.

These electrons may be the outer electrons of the atoms in the crystal lattice, or they may be electrons associated with defects in the lattice. Defects in the lattice which cause colour are called *colour centres* or F-centres (from the German, *Farbe*). These centres are lattice defects that absorb light. Such defects may be due to:

(1) The presence of foreign atoms in the lattice
(2) An excess of atoms of one element over that required by the chemical formula, for example, an excess of calcium atoms in a crystal of fluorite (CaF_2)
(3) Mechanical deformation of the lattice

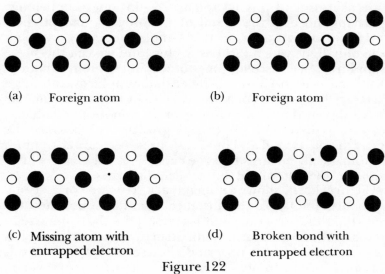

(a)   Foreign atom

(b)   Foreign atom

(c)   Missing atom with
      entrapped electron

(d)   Broken bond with
      entrapped electron

Figure 122

To see how the presence of foreign atoms in the structure causes colour we look first at a hypothetical section of the mineral, corundum (Al_2O_3), seen in Figure 122a. In the first instance, we see that an atom of chromium has substituted in the structure for an atom of aluminium. Chromium and aluminium atoms are approximately the same size, and the chromium will fit into the corundum structure in place of an aluminium atom — almost. As it turns out, the chromium atom is just slightly larger than the aluminium atom, and fitting it into the structure is rather like putting a size 6 foot into a size 5½ shoe — it will fit, but it pinches! The 'pinch' in this case is a disturbance of the bond energy surrounding the chromium atom, causing a slight distortion in the crystal lattice. It is this disturbance that frees electrons from one position and entraps them in others. These entrapped electrons then absorb the energy of certain wavelengths of light that pass through it, and in the case of chromium in the corundum structure, the only wavelength that 'escapes' is red, thus producing a corundum that is red to the eye which we call ruby.

Exactly how the electron 'traps' energy is not known: as one professor of physics remarked, this question belongs perhaps more to the realm of philosophy than physics.

If the foreign atom in this same structure is titanium, the only light which escapes is blue, and we call the stone sapphire. We discover one other interesting situation. Rubies are almost always smaller than sapphires, and there are very few large rubies known in the world. Experiments have shown that chromium, even in minute percentages, causes a disruption in crystal growth and inhibits the growth of crystals. Thus the presence of chromium automatically ensures that the crystal it is colouring will be smaller than it would have been otherwise.

Figure 122b, shows an imaginary structure of a crystal of quartz (SiO_2). In this instance, iron has substituted for silicon in the structure, but it is not quite the same size as the silicon. Once again, slight structural deformation has taken place in the lattice and the freed electrons in this instance are trapping all of the colours except violet, turning this piece of quartz into amethyst.

Sometimes, although a particular crystal has entrapped foreign atoms, until some outside agency such as heat or radiation is applied to the crystal there is no colour change. An example of this is quartz, where an occasional aluminium atom has substituted for a silicon atom. Unless this crystal has grown in an area where there is a certain amount of natural radioactivity in the rocks, the crystal will remain colourless. But if it is subjected to even a relatively small amount of radiation, the crystal will assume a range of colours from yellow brown to black (citrine and smoky quartz).

Many gemstones are regularly heat treated to change their colour, and within the last decade certain gems such as diamonds have had their colours changed by irradiation with X-rays. In both of these treatments, when foreign atoms are present, there seems to be a change of energy state in the foreign atom, freeing extra electrons to absorb different wavelengths of light. An example of this is brown zircon, which is regularly heat treated to turn it blue. There are also certain varieties of amethyst that can be heat treated to turn them yellow-brown (citrine).

The amount of foreign atoms that it takes to cause coloration is relatively small — only a few atoms out of every million normal atoms. How little it takes can be easily imagined by visualizing a cube of quartz a foot on each side, and realizing that the amount of iron that it would take to turn that cube into amethyst is approximately the amount of iron in the head of a pin.

The second of our situations producing F-centres is that of an excess of one element over that required by the chemical formula. This is not a particularly common type of coloration and seems to occur mostly in crystals with ionic bonding. Once again the extra atoms cause lattice deformations that trap light absorbing electrons.

The third colour-causing situation is deformation of the crystal lattice. This can be produced mechanically by pressure or by heating. Generally speaking, any disturbance of the lattice will produce vacant positions for the positively and negatively charged atoms. The absence of a negative charge behaves electrically like a positive charge and can capture an electron. These types of F-centres are believed to be a positively charged vacancy, with an electron moving about in it. Another type of lattice defect that falls into this category is an incomplete (broken) bond which can also serve as an electron trap. Both of these situations are seen in Figures 122c and 122d. These stressed lattices and their ability to trap electrons behave very much like the stresses caused by foreign atoms in the first example.

When colour is produced in an initially colourless crystal

by irradiating it, it is supposed that some of the atoms have lost an outer electron which has absorbed a quantity of energy, thus allowing it to move about freely. If the lattice were perfect, it would fall back again when the excitation ceased, but lattice defects provide local energy levels into which the electron can move. When irradiation ceases, the energy distribution in the crystal will have been changed and F centres that absorb light energy will have been formed. The crystal will now be coloured.

Each positively charged atom that has lost an electron will now have a vacancy in its outer energy level. Such atoms are called positive holes — a term used much in connection with transistors — and will have the power to capture any new electrons that come along.

Let us now sum up what we have learned about energy behaviour in crystals thus far in this chapter. If mechanical energy is put into a crystal, either by striking a blow, or by squeezing it, the crystal gives off light and electricity. If the process is reversed and electricity is put into the crystal, mechanical energy (vibration) results. If heat energy is put into a crystal, electrical energy results. In coloured crystals, when white light is put into a crystal its energy changes, and only light of a certain wavelength (colour) escapes.

In each instance, then, the energy that goes in is not the same as the energy that comes out. In other words, energy has been *transformed*. Therefore, we see the principle benefit of the use of crystals — that they are *transformers* of energy.

Having examined the transformative power of crystals with mundane energies, let us now turn our attention to spiritual energies and see how they behave.

Spiritual Energies
In understanding the relationship between crystals and spiritual energy, we must look into levels of energy that are not directly measurable by scientific methods. When we look into this level of energy, we discover that the *elemental* energy of the crystal becomes most important. But what is elemental energy? For that matter, what exactly is *energy*?

In the previous portion of this chapter we have

discussed some of the effects of energy, but we have not established what it *is*. Nor can we do so. Scientists have become very adept at describing the behaviour and effects of energy, but we still have no real idea exactly what energy is. The scientifically inclined will probably find the following discussion of elementals a little 'far out', but when we talk about beings made of energy we are talking no less scientifically than the physicist who talks about the effects of gravity, but who has very little idea about what gravity *is*.

We know that elementals exist behind every physical form, and we might perhaps define them as the *essence* behind the form. There are other names which have also been applied to these essential forms such as Deva (a Sanskrit word meaning 'a being of light'), or even Angelic beings.

We have already begun to see through Kirlian photography that certain energy forms exist where no physical form is present. In a famous experiment, a Kirlian photograph was taken of a frog, and then one of the legs was removed from the body. Another photograph was taken, and the energy form was exactly the same as if the missing limb had been present. In other words, the photograph showed the *energy* of the leg as still being present, although in physical form it was missing.

We know that elementals are present in the plant and animal kingdoms, and many instances have been reported of being able to contact these elementals telepathically. The classic example of this is the contact with such beings by Dorothy Maclean at the Findhorn community in Scotland in the early days of that community. Other such contacts are also well documented in esoteric literature. Many of you will also be familiar with the experiments done a few years ago in connecting instruments called polygraphs (lie detectors) to plants and then directing either friendly or hostile thoughts towards them, and noting that plants respond very differently to different types of thought. In another classic experiment several plants were connected to polygraphs, and one was burned with a cigarette. The next day, *all* of the plants in the room registered a very strong fear reaction as the experimenter merely entered the room.

Experiments such as these have demonstrated in particular that the plant kingdom has awareness. We have always recognized that the animal kingdom is aware to varying degrees, but what we are only now beginning to realize is that the *mineral kingdom* also has awareness. Admittedly, it is not on the same level as the awareness of the other kingdoms, but it is awareness none the less. And with awareness goes a certain degree of free will. We have often thought of the kingdom of man as being the only kingdom having free will, but we can quickly demonstrate that the other kingdoms have free will, although again it is a matter of degree.

A rather simple example will demonstrate the various degrees of free will available to members of the various kingdoms.

If a man is out in the bright sun, and wishes to cool off, he can simply move into the shade. Or he may shed some clothes or put up an umbrella, or perhaps build a swimming pool or invent the air conditioner. The list is endless.

If an animal is unhappy in the hot sunlight it can choose to move to a shady place, or perhaps sit in a lake or stream. Going one stage lower, if a plant is unhappy in bright sun (or desires even *more* sun) it cannot move from place to place, but it may slightly alter its direction of growth or roll up its leaves, or close its flowers to alter the amount of sunlight it receives. It has less choice. But what of the mineral kingdom? If a stone is sitting in a place where it does not desire to be (if the term desire even applies at that level of awareness), then it must sit there until some other agency comes along to move it. In other words, the mineral kingdom is largely dependent on the will of others, and has little free will of its own. Now if we remember that the elemental is the essence of the particular kingdom, then we must also realize that the elementals of the mineral kingdom have little free will of their own by their very nature. It is this lack of free will and their susceptibility to direction by other, higher levels of will that make them so very powerful when combined with one *other* factor.

Wherever you are sitting right now, look around you. In your field of view, you may see representatives of the plant kingdom, and perhaps a few representatives of the animal kingdom, and you yourself are a representative of the kingdom of man. The physical forms of all of these kingdoms are present and therefore the elemental energies of these kingdoms are present. Also present in one form or another is the elemental presence of the mineral kingdom. In fact, the very planet on which you are sitting is made up of the mineral kingdom. But what happens if you go to the moon? Or Mars? There are no plants. There are no animals. The kingdom of man is not represented. In other words, the elementals of these kingdoms are not present, or if they are present, they are not very strongly manifested. But what we *do* find in every instance, is the mineral kingdom. And the minerals that we find on other planetary bodies are exactly the same as those that we find on the Earth. The elemental energies of the mineral kingdom are *universal* energies. And, therefore, when we contact this energy, and begin to exercise our own creativity with this energy through our own exercise of Higher Will, we are drawing on the very energies around which the physical universe is made. This is why crystals are so very powerful and also why their powers and energies must only be used through the individual user's highest consciousness.*

Remember that the efforts described at the beginning of this chapter relating to the physical form of the crystal are also related to the elemental energy of the crystal. We described the physical energies of the crystal as being in

*We know that the minerals throughout the universe are the same as those on Earth through studies not only of Moon rocks but of thousands of meteorites which have fallen onto the Earth, and which, for the most part, have identical minerals to those on the Earth. Those minerals discovered in meteorites that are not found on the Earth are found in such minute proportions that they may very well be present on the Earth and we have not yet discovered them. There are several new minerals discovered each year.

perfect balance, but it is important to remember that *all* of the energies of the crystal are in perfect balance, both the spiritual and the physical, and that all of these energies are in perfect and natural harmony. Thus in the crystal we discover the perfect natural balance between physical and spiritual energy. When energy passes through a natural crystal, it becomes harmonized with it, and the natural balance is preserved. It is this tendency of crystals to balance energy that provides the mechanism through which transformation takes place, and this natural tendency of crystals to transform energy applies at spiritual as well as the mundane levels of energy.

It is this ability of crystals to transform and harmonize energies at all levels that is their greatest power and potential for use.

In practical terms, if the energies embodied by the user of the crystal are not quite in balance and harmony, there will be a natural tendency in the crystal to correct and rebalance any energies that the person sends through the crystal. This, then, is a tendency to focus more precisely the user's energy, and often gives the impression that the crystal has increased or amplified this energy. Remember that the crystal does not increase the energy of the user: it merely focuses it, and in some instances adds to it.

But how can a crystal add to the user's energy? The answer is in the environment in which we live — a planet made principally of the mineral kingdom, and with other kingdoms existing on it that have evolved from the mineral kingdom. The natural tendency of the mineral kingdom is to create perfect balance and harmony, and this elemental energy is largely directed by Higher Will. The outworking of Higher Will on the Earth is through the race of Man, yet from the end of Atlantean times through to the present, this will has been to draw to itself as much disharmony as possible, through the outworking of the Laws of Karma. But the coming of the New Age is a time when we seek to redress the imbalances in the Earth Being and all kingdoms that dwell upon it (which we call 'healing'), which is exactly what crystals wish to do by their own nature. When we enlist the aid of the mineral kingdom to help us reharmonize the Earth, be it by healing individual human beings, healing the environment or healing the physical body of the Earth itself, we are coming back into step with the natural order of things, which gives just that much more thrust to our own Creative Will.

So, by enlisting the energies of the mineral kingdom through its most precise form, the crystal, we can, through our own act of will, enlist the aid of these elemental energies in our planetary healing. The crystal has no free will of its own, so it cannot create harmony in levels of awareness higher than its own without the influence of higher will. When we use a crystal with will (or intention) we are merely directing the elemental energy of the crystal to aid us in our own creativity.

Through the elemental of the crystal we can also draw additional elemental energy that is in harmony with our own. But unless we produce an energy of will, and give that energy of will some of our own essence of creativity, the elemental will produce no energy at all. Practical applications of this energy of will working in harmony with the elemental energy will be discussed in the following chapters.

One last point to mention — that each and every crystal will have its own individual energy, just as every human being or plant or animal has their own individual energy. This is largely dependent on the natural environment in which the crystal grows, and since every natural environment is somewhat different from the next, every crystal will be somewhat different from the next, especially at elemental level, where each crystal may be said to have its own 'personality' much as every human being has their own individual personality. In simple terms, every crystal is different from every other crystal.

This can easily be demonstrated in a workshop environment, and experiments for discovering this are discussed in a later chapter.

On a slightly larger scale, we will discover that crystals from one location on the Earth will differ considerably in subtle energies from otherwise identical crystals from some other place on the earth. For example, quartz crystals from Brazil can be physically identical to quartz crystals from Arkansas in the USA, but even a relatively unaware person will be able to sense that their energies are considerably different from one another.

In the following chapters, then, we shall begin to explore our own relationship with the elementals of crystals, and discover how these energies can be used in co-operation and harmony for healing the Earth.

Balance and harmony are the things most lacking in the world today; and yet we live on a world that is *made* of crystals, with their natural tendency for harmony. Some-one once calculated (and the writer has checked it) that the entire human race could fit into a half-mile (.8 kilometre) cube. If there are any doubts about the ability of mankind to influence the Earth Being in a positive way, we need only look around us to see how much disharmony this minute fragment of the whole of the Earth Being has caused. But the potential for harmony is there also, and perhaps with this perspective of how much of the physical Earth we occupy, we can begin to see how only a small portion of mankind working for the good of the planet can create changes far out of proportion to our numbers — especially when combined with the universal power of crystals.

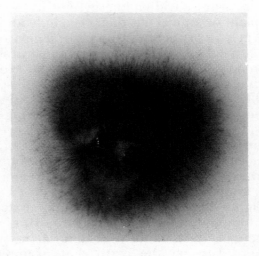

Figure 123   Fluorite

Through Kirlian photography we are beginning to accumulate evidence about unseen energies of all kinds. I have taken Kirlian photographs of various crystals, several of which are included herein. The interpretation of these is still in question, revolving around the basic question of what *is* energy. This leaves some doubt as to what we are actually photographing, but nonetheless there are several obvious things about them.

First, they are all different. It has been proven that each individual crystal produces an identical pattern each time it is photographed, as long as the conditions are the same. Therefore, we are not just seeing variations on the same theme.

Second, the patterns produced have within themselves important differences. For example, the fluorite crystals in Figures 123 and 124 both show well developed stringers of energy, while the rock crystal in Figure 126 shows almost no stringer development, and has mostly diffused the energy.

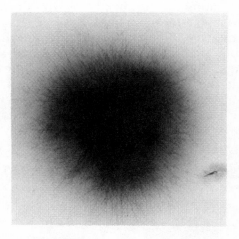

Figure 124   Fluorite

Also in Figures 123 and 124 the octahedron of fluorite only has one face actually in contact with the paper (the centre triangle), but the other three faces on that side of the octahedron have left a very distinct imprint. This may

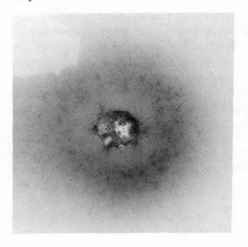

Figure 125   Aquamarine, looking down 'C' axis

be due to the ionic bonding of the fluorite, allowing an electron flow along the atomic planes, and flowing straight out of the crystal faces.

The aquamarine, Figure 125, has diffused the energy to a degree, but there are still well-developed stringers at certain points. The lighter 'shadow' around the crystal is of interest, but the exact meaning is unknown.

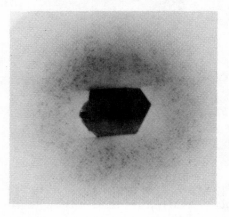

Figure 126   Rock crystal, looking down 'C' axis

This same type of shadow appears in the rock crystal in Figures 126 and 127, but it is interesting to note that in Figure 126, taken along the 'C' axis, the shadowing does not occur on two sides of the crystal, while in Figure 127, taken perpendicular to the 'C' axis, it again extends all around. This may be related to the direction and strength of the atomic bonding.

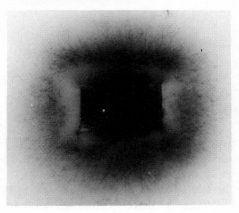

Figure 127   Same crystal as Figure 126, but perpendicular to 'C' axis

In the following chapters, we will look at ways in which crystal energy may be used. Perhaps these photographs will at least demonstrate to the sceptical that *something* is happening.

8.

Uses of Crystals

Preparing to Use Crystals
The use of crystals involves several distinct stages. The first of these is *acquiring* crystals.

Although it is enjoyable to find your own crystals if and when possible, this is, unfortunately, difficult for many people. Not all areas of the Earth are blessed with good collecting areas, although it is surprising what is available in your own neighbourhood. You can find out by making enquiries at your local museum, or through geological societies, or even the Geology or Earth Science departments of a nearby university. You may also be able to find guide books written for the collector which describe various collecting localities. Such books are often available through mineral dealers as well. If you happen to live in or near a city with a book store dealing in textbooks of various sorts, you may very well find some interesting guide books tucked away in areas of the book shop dealing with geology and mineralogy.

In a number of countries, there are clubs for people who collect rocks and minerals. These clubs will have knowledge of, and access to, many good collecting locations. Enquire about such clubs through mineral dealers, or try the Yellow Pages. These clubs are very popular in Australia, New Zealand and the USA.

If you are fortunate enough to live in or near an area

where mining or quarrying has taken place, there are excellent possibilities for finding crystals in the waste rock from both types of operations. Always be certain you have permission from the landowner or mine operator to collect, and be aware that these types of locations can be extremely hazardous. Under no circumstances should you enter mine tunnels or underground workings, as they are often quite unstable, and cave-ins and rockfalls can happen quite easily. Also be quite cautious when walking in such areas, as vertical shafts will often be overgrown and difficult to see until it is too late. If you take children into such areas, keep them in sight (and within easy reach) at all times.

The types of crystals that can be found in such locations are many and varied, although not all mines or quarries will produce specimens. Take a small hammer and chisel along with you for separating crystals from the adhering rock, and also take along a container of some sort to carry them back in. Don't depend on your pockets — they get full all too soon.

Whenever you are in the countryside where rocks are exposed, look out for any changes in appearance in the rocks, especially changes in coloration which appear as straight lines or streaks. Often these will be veins of a differing mineral, and can contain crystals.

Beaches and stream beds are also good places to find all sorts of rocks and minerals, although they are much more likely to be water rounded. This does not necessarily detract from their usefulness as spiritual instruments, and once again your own sensitivity and awareness will tell you which ones want to come home with you. If you have been drawn to this book, you may already have piles of rocks and crystals on every available shelf. When you make friends with minerals, they all want to come home with you, it seems.

The most common method of acquiring crystals is to buy them. There is certainly nothing wrong with this, since you are simply exchanging the energy you have put into acquiring your money for the energy that the crystal has accumulated in making its way to you. A crystal that has come half way around the world has acquired the energy of the miner, of the buyer, of the importer, and of the various forms of transportation required to reach the mineral seller. The exchange for money energy maintains the perfect balance of energy that characterizes a crystal.

As to where crystals can be purchased, the yellow pages of your local telephone directory is a good place to begin. Depending on the part of the world in which you live there will be several types of headings to look for. These may be entitled *Rock Shops, Minerals for Collectors, Lapidary Equipment and Supplies, Mineralogists*. Many of the businesses listed under these categories will not have crystals available for sale, but they will probably know where you can enquire further in your local area. If you do not happen to live in a large town, it is possible that you will find none of these listings in your local yellow pages. If not, try to locate the yellow pages for the largest town near you and begin there. You may need to make a number of enquiries.

Crystals can often be purchased by post, but it is most desirable to make your own choice in person. The actual method of deciding which crystal (or crystals) is the right one is simple — only choose what you are drawn to. Forget that you are a Taurian or a Libran and that some book or other says you should have such and such a stone. You are a unique individual and each crystal is a unique individual. Remember that this uniqueness is part of the subtle makeup of both you and the crystal, and the only way such energies can be sensed is through the intuition.

Many people feel that they are not very intuitive, but almost every one of us has had an experience of a 'first impression' — something inside us that tells us there is something about a person or place that does not tally with what we are being told, or perhaps with what we feel we *should* be feeling about that person or place. Later events almost always prove the 'first impression' to have been correct. This is really nothing more than a flash of intuition — which our 'thinking' mind later talks us out of.

Many readers will already have confidence in their intuitive ability, but for those who do not, what might be called the 'first impression method' is suggested.

It is very easy — just stand in front of a group of crystals, shut your eyes and relax, then open your eyes quickly, and grab the first crystal that your eye is drawn to! This crystal will almost always be the one that is needed at that moment. In that instant, before the thinking mind can react, the intuition (which is almost instantaneous) has already flashed to the right one.

If you are choosing crystals for a specific purpose such as healing or meditation, then have this purpose in mind, or even project it to the crystals, and see which one responds, which one you are drawn to. Some people will actually sense an energy response from a particular crystal, perhaps as a flash of light, a vibration, or even a sense of the crystal almost jumping up and down saying 'ME! — ME! — ME!'

Sometimes it is not possible to choose crystals in person, or you may be asked, or feel drawn, to choose a crystal for someone else. There is nothing wrong with this, as long, again, as you choose intuitively. A good method is to visualize the person for whom you are choosing the crystal, project that visualization to the crystals, and see which one responds.

Occasionally you may be drawn to a particular crystal without knowing why. It may be that if that crystal is for you, it is for sometime in the future. This may be the only chance you and the crystal have to meet: when the crystal is finally needed it may not be possible to be physically present in the same place. Alternatively, the crystal may be for someone else — perhaps someone you have not even met yet, and you have the opportunity to acquire the crystal that they may not have. Again, the intuition takes care of these situations.

If you are given a crystal, or are not sure why a particular crystal has been drawn to you (or you to it), meditation may provide the answer. This will be covered later on in this chapter.

It is sometimes tempting to have someone else choose a crystal for us, someone who supposedly 'knows' more than we do about them. *Always* choose for yourself — anyone who chooses for you has taken away from you the opportunity to expand your own awareness and intuition. Your guidance or inner feelings for yourself are *always* better than someone else's you.

One last thing — there are several magazines published in the USA, with international distribution, that are dedicated entirely to the mineral collector. Two of these are *The Lapidary Journal*, and *Gems and Minerals*. An enquiry at your nearest science museum could also produce the names of journals available in your local area. In these magazines there are many advertisements for crystals of all types, and information will be available about places to collect your own crystals.

Consecration

The second stage of crystal use could be called *consecration* or *protection*.

The protection of crystal energies against misuse is extremely important and will become even more important in the future. We must keep in mind that the forces of the crystal can be made to do the work of the dark as well as the light. Therefore it is necessary to protect all crystals that come into contact with us against deliberate misuse. Since crystals respond to the energy of will, it is enough just to hold the crystal and will that the crystal will be used for no purpose that is not of the highest. The crystal can even be programmed so that the protection cannot be removed by anyone — including the user! This is especially important for crystals that are used by groups, and it may be necessary for one member of the group to be responsible for the crystal and to make sure that the protection is constantly maintained.

Cleansing

Since crystals are used primarily in dealing with subtle energies, and since these energies tend to have an effect on the very nature of the matter that makes up the crystals, it will be necessary to cleanse them occasionally of any undesirable energy. This process really begins with the acquiring of a crystal, because you will have little knowledge of who has handled it, or what energies it has been exposed to before it came into your hands. There is a certain amount of subtle energy already programmed into your crystal that is a result of the natural environment in which it grew. Although this is not usually apparent in its physical form, with experience of discerning energies you will be able to tell a piece of quartz crystal that has come from Arkansas in the USA, from a Brazilian one. In one you will find a very clear and high energy, in the other a much more diffused and less intense energy. Remember that in choosing your crystal in the first place, your intuitive reaction will automatically compensate for differences in the original growing environment, and you will always get exactly the one that grew in the environment necessary to harmonize with your own particular energy.

In the process of cleansing a newly acquired crystal we want to leave in all the natural energies and take out any of the energies it has accumulated since that time. Remembering that crystals respond to the intention of the user, it is enough just to intend that these natural energies remain, and they will. What to do with energies that you have deliberately placed in the crystal, and wish to retain, is discussed later on.

The actual technique of cleansing varies from individual to individual, and you will find a technique through experimentation that will feel right for you. There are several techniques that have proven to be effective.

First, you can just wash them in flowing water. Water is a universal cleanser and is effective in cleaning those energies that are undesirable in the physical body, whether it be the body of a person or the body of a crystal. Many of you are familiar with the effect of salt water in cleansing your own body's aura, and a similar effect is seen on the 'aura' of a crystal. A word of caution though — do not use hot water on your crystals, as it is likely to shatter them. Always use water that feels cool to the touch, or cold water. You will find that even at room temperature, your crystals will feel cool to the touch, and the water temperature should match that feel as nearly as possible. During the actual washing of the crystal, it should be held in the hand, and the holder should will or intend that all energies not desired in the crystal will be washed away and that all desirable energies will remain. It is also worth asking the elementals of water to accept these negative energies, and to transform them into positive energies. And always thank them for doing so.

Sunlight is always a great cleanser, and if it is possible or practical to do so, leave your crystals in the sunlight, once again with the intention of cleansing any negative energies, and also with the intention of transforming those negative energies into positive. A few hours should be sufficient, but allow your own sensitivities to be the judge.

Some people suggest washing crystals in eucalyptus oil or surgical spirit (medical alcohol), or even breathing on them in a certain manner. Truly, it does not matter: in each instance, it is the intention of the user to clean the crystal, and it is this intention to which the crystal responds.

An equally effective and rapid method is the visualization method. In this method, the crystal is held or cupped between the hands and the user visualizes positive energy flowing through the crystal, sweeping away all negative or undesirable energies. One method that is particularly effective is to visualize a flow of perfectly clear and pure mountain spring water flowing through the crystal, sweeping away all impurities, at the same time transforming them into some positive energy, such as light or love. In this visualization you are getting some additional help from the elemental energies of water, which you are invoking through the visualization.

Note that, not only were the undesirable energies taken out of the crystal, but once removed they were transformed into other, more positive energies. No matter what type of cleansing is done, there is no point in removing negative energies and scattering them willy nilly about the Earth. Unless they are transformed, they will simply go elsewhere, and become someone else's problem. Since the cleansing of the Earth of its negativity is the prime objective of all workers for the light, it is pointless to send them off elsewhere.

The question of programming crystals — that is, of putting thoughts and energies into crystals that you wish them to retain — will be covered in the next section, but, obviously, we do not wish to remove these particular thought patterns from the crystal. Therefore, during the cleansing process, we need to intend that all programming we have put into the crystal is also retained. The question of when to clean crystals apart from the initial cleansing will largely depend on the intuition of the user, as well as on the use to which they are put. Crystals that are being intensely used, such as those used by a healer on a regular daily basis, will need frequent cleansing. It will probably be necessary to clean healing crystals each morning before the first patient so that any energies accumulated overnight will be removed, as well as between each patient. This is so that energies from other patients will not be passed on to the next. It is also possible to programme into your crystal a 'self-cleaning' programme, whereby the crystal will automatically rid itself of negative energies as they accumulate. Once again, a little experimentation on the part of the individual user will determine the best method.

Certain crystals such as amethysts seem to have a natural ability to pull negative energies from the air. This is why many spiritual groups who have a common room for meditation will often be intuitively drawn to having a large cluster of amethysts in the room. Such crystals should be cleansed frequently and such groups of crystals are used like 'spiritual room-fresheners'.

Programming
Programming is the process of instructing the elemental of the crystal how to use its tendency to transform, balance and harmonize energy. It is not unlike programming a computer, because unless you give the elemental precise directions, the response will be less than total. This is one beneficial 'side effect' for the crystal user — as you use crystals, you must also become 'crystal clear' in your own use of energies.

The act of picking up a crystal with the intention of using it for a particular activity is the simplest form of programming. It is not really necessary to consciously programme all crystals, especially those carried for personal use whenever a need should arise. In this instance, the crystal is 'programmed' as it is used, and it is not desired that the crystal should retain the programme. It could be said that such a crystal is already programmed with the user's own energy, but this often takes place at an unconscious level.

Crystals that are used for a single purpose, such as healing or meditation, benefit most from conscious programming, where it is desired that the crystal should retain its programme. The actual process is simple. All that is necessary is to direct a thought into the particular crystal, intending that that crystal's energies should be focused for a particular purpose and that the crystal should retain that particular thought or intention within itself. During this process it is most effective for the crystal to be held in the hand of the user, since this will help the crystal to harmonize totally with all the mundane energies of the electrical 'aura', as well as with the highest spiritual consciousness. All of this will be imprinted in the crystal during the process of programming. The laws of spirit prevent the user from drawing through his crystal levels of spiritual energy that are higher than those the user can handle. Thus, the user is protected to a large extent from opening spiritual doors he cannot close. Nonetheless, it is prudent to have in mind' when programming your crystal that you do not want any energies that you cannot handle, but still leave the door open for higher levels of energy to come through the crystal as your own personal level of awareness increases.

Before going on to describe techniques of use, there are one or two other points. Many users feel that personal crystals, that is, crystals that are used solely by one person, are best kept out of sight and not handled by others. This is so that the large amount of personal energy involved with such a crystal is not disrupted. Such crystals often like to be kept in a dark place, such as a bag of black, blue or purple velvet, when not in use.

Where others' energies are involved, crystals in general use (such as healing crystals) are often happy to be on display and to be handled by anyone. Again, your individual intuition will tell you how your crystals want to be kept.

Some crystals are happy with certain other crystals, and not so happy with others. This probably has to do with the harmony (or lack of it) of their natural energies. Thus some crystals will feel content next to one another on a shelf, and some will not. In either case, it is no reflection on the crystals involved — it just is as it is. In using crystals there will probably be one direction or another that the crystal will naturally point. Different teachers say that the termination should point in this direction or that direction. In the experience of the writer with many workshop groups, there is no particular rule about this except that there will be a certain way that some crystals will feel natural in the hand, but that it varies greatly from person to person, so go by whatever feels right to you.

Contacting Crystal Energy

The purpose of this section is not to provide a list of techniques and uses to select from, but rather to show a few of the ways in which crystals have been used, as a guide to begin developing personal techniques. The subject of healing, both personal and planetary, is one of the major crystal uses and will be discussed later.

Our work with crystals goes hand in hand with our own spiritual awakening — the process of gradually raising the total spectrum of personal energy from the densest, and most material, to the highest and most spiritual. As you progress from point to point in this awakening process, your own total energy make-up, or vibration, undergoes a change.

As you become more and more aware and awake spiritually, and as your own particular vibration changes, different crystals come into your life to correspond and harmonize with those vibrations. Let us remember that a crystal is an expression of universal consciousness and that as a particular crystal, also part of that universal consciousness, begins to correspond and harmonize with our particular energy, we can find through the crystal a gateway to our own process of realization, a point of contact with the Universal Mind. It is also true that a particular crystal which was 'ours' at a particular time of our life may not be so in the future. Therefore, let us look on crystals as spiritual tools, and not as possessions. And, when our work with a particular tool is finished, we lay it down and go onto the next appropriate tool. We do not discard it, but rather pass it on to someone else who needs it. You can be certain that when you are finished with a particular crystal in your life, the Universal Consciousness will make absolutely certain that the next person who needs that tool will be drawn to you. It is then up to you to recognise this fact and pass the crystal on in an appropriate manner to the person who needs it. There is certainly nothing wrong with selling it, if this is appropriate. The pattern of the universe involves exchange of energy, and money is certainly a valid form of energy. On the other hand, it may be totally inappropriate — by the time you have developed your sensitivity sufficiently to know that you are finished with a particular crystal, you will also have sensitivity to know the appropriate method of transferring it to its next user.

All seekers will find that crystals, when added to various forms and techniques for expanding awareness, will serve to focus the energies through the various forms.

The first point of contact with crystal energies is through meditation.

Remember that the crystal is a perfect expression of the divine mind. The crystal cannot grow without a programme, and that programme is part of the divine mind itself. When you tune in to the energy of the crystal, you are tuning in to a very precise aspect of the divine mind.

Since crystals put you in touch with a high aspect of divinity you are aided in your meditation to reach higher and higher levels, and it is in those levels where you begin to discover the divinity within yourself. In doing so it may seem that the crystal has magnified your own energy, but it has merely focused it.

There is a great deal of information about the mineral kingdom that can be gleaned from meditation, and indeed, a great deal of information is also available on the very nature of matter. All workers for the spirit who are seriously interested in the process of bringing spirit into matter should consider meditation as a method of contacting the higher intelligence of crystals and matter in order to begin to sense your own personal role in this process, to begin to make contact with the Elemental or Devic force of the crystal.

A word of caution about such contacts though — the

Elemental of a particular substance or object has no interest other than that particular object, and will speak only from that standpoint. It will be up to you as a co-creator with the universe to ensure that any actions which you take as a result of such a devic contact are in harmony with the overall planetary picture. Obviously this requires a great deal of attunement on the part of the user.

During such a meditation it is wise, at least in the beginning, to meditate on the crystal, rather than attempt to go *into* the crystal. The more you become intimately involved with the energy structure of the crystal by going into it, the closer your contact with the elemental energy becomes, and the more difficult it becomes to assess the information received, from a point of detachment. In such a meditation, always let your inbuilt sense of 'rightness' and 'wrongness' be your guide.

Crystals can also be used as an aid to other types of meditation, as crystals of certain minerals seem to have a very calming effect. In workshop sensitivity training, a significant number of people will find the mineral aquamarine to have a calming effect, for example. A smaller percentage of participants will feel the same sort of calming effect with other minerals, so once again it is totally up to the intuition of the individual as to which crystal is appropriate.

The actual meditation technique can be nothing more than holding a crystal in your hand, or in some instances crystals of different minerals in each hand. Or you can place a crystal on the floor in front of you, or on a small table where you can focus on it as you meditate.

In this process of using crystals in meditation, the crystal, by its very nature, must respond to the intent of the user and induce an energy that is complementary to meditation.

Another interesting technique is to have a number of crystals placed in a circle on the floor, with the meditator sitting in the centre of the circle. The actual choice of crystals for this process is quite personal, but they can all be of one mineral, such as quartz, or perhaps a mixture of different minerals. This technique of forming a circle of crystals can also be used to 'charge' another crystal by placing it in the centre of the circle.

It is often a good idea to meditate with a newly acquired crystal, especially if you are not clear on why it has come to you. In this meditation, ask the crystal what uses it is in harmony with and what it would like to be used for. The response may be an intuitive feeling, a vision of a particular use, or perhaps even a sensation of a 'verbal' reply. Just leave your mind open to whatever happens.

But how can an inanimate object tell us anything? Again, we are contacting the living intelligence behind the physical form of the crystal.

Group meditations can also be enhanced through the use of crystals; once again, sitting in a circle is usually the most effective technique. There are several possibilities for the introduction of crystals into such a meditation. Many groups use a large single crystal in the centre of the circle, as the focus of the group energy. Alternatively, each person in the group may bring their own crystal and hold them throughout the meditation.

When crystals are used in a group it is often wise to discuss beforehand, and make perfectly clear to the members, the precise intention of the group, particularly if a single large crystal is being used. The energy of intention directed into that crystal is then focused as clearly and precisely as possible. If every person in the group has a differing idea and intent, in many instances the energies will just cancel each other out. Also, when a crystal is used by a group for *any* purpose it is particularly important that it should be protected against conscious or unconscious misuse. Many groups who use such crystals often appoint a particular person (or one person feels drawn) to act as 'guardian' of the crystal responsible for cleaning and protecting the crystal. Crystals in group use should have their protective programming reinforced periodically, as the determined efforts (often unseen and unsensed) of a person in the group deliberately misusing the energies of the crystal and of the group can often wear down or confuse the positive energies. However, if the group is highly attuned and working for a high purpose, the chances of this happening are slight, but the possibility should always be borne in mind.

There are also numerous people who meditate in pyramids. A crystal placed at either the apex of the pyramid or at the energy focus can be quite powerful. This is not a technique recommended for beginners, however, as the energy of the crystal combined with the energy of the pyramid requires a great deal of conscious high attunement, and particularly a great deal of clarity of purpose, in order to control it correctly. This is definitely not the place for the unaware and unawakened to experiment.

Crystals are particularly responsive to music — sound waves produced by compression of air (mechanical energy). We will recall from Chapter 7 that when you compress a crystal, energy is generated. The energies are slight, but it is this level of energy that the intuitive mind is particularly aware of. You will find that holding a crystal during meditation with music will often produce some quite startling effects, and in many instances you will be able to 'see' the music in terms of colour or shape. Even if you are just listening to music and not in a meditative state, you will find the depth of experience of the music greatly enhanced by the presence of a crystal. When harmonious music is played in the presence of a crystal, much of the intention of the composer is impressed in the crystal structure, and if you 'listen' to the crystal afterwards in a meditative state you will often be able to pick up the etheric message of the music. If you happen to be a singer, try singing to your crystal and see what happens. If you have a piano, play single notes to a crystal and see how the response varies.

Manifestation is another spiritual activity that can benefit from the addition of crystals to the usual techniques. This is one area, though, where a very fine line is drawn between aiding the universe to give you what you really need and forcing it to give you what you want. It is worth remembering that unfulfilled want is one of the real sources of unhappiness of life, and if you want something desperately enough and are unable to obtain it in this lifetime, you may keep drawing yourself into further lifetimes until the want is fulfilled.

Need, on the other hand, will always be fulfilled as long

as you do not block it with too much 'want'. Those things which we truly need are those which fulfil our own particular plan for the present incarnation. It may be asked: 'If it's truly a need, won't it come anyway?'

The answer to that question can be best stated in old proverb, 'God feeds every sparrow, but He doesn't throw worms into the nest'. Your needs will always be fulfilled, but you may have to work very hard for them!

We know that the energy of will to fulfill need sets in motion events on several spiritual planes and it is in these planes of energy that crystals can be of use. It is through the energy of will, or the intention to draw to yourself what you need to fulfil your plan, that, when directed through a crystal, can produce an energy appropriate to the fulfilment of that need. In a sense, you are broadcasting that energy into a higher plane and the direct connection of the material plane (the crystal) to the higher planes can help to create a stronger and more positive response.

Crystals can also be used in conjuction with the plant kingdom. For example, if you have problems in the garden, put a perfect image of the garden into the crystal, and place or bury the crystal in an appropriate spot in the garden. Again, your own sensitivity will tell you where the crystal wants to be, and the direction in which it wishes to face. Do you have an ill plant, either in the garden or in the house? Why not fill the crystal full of healing energy and leave it next to the plant. Or, why not programme a crystal with the vital energies of plant growth, and plant one with seeds in the Spring.

Likewise, a crystal may be programmed to help neutralize harmful chemicals in processed food. In this instance, you are de-programming the molecular links that bind the harmful substance together. Remember, though, to transmute the harmful substances into helpful ones.

Yet another use of crystals that has yet to be fully explored is in combination with the particular technique in crop growing, known as *Genesics*. Genesics involves planting in circles rather than rows, and is proving to be a very useful technique for all sorts of food crops. By the use of the circle, the natural energy of the plants is retained in a continuous flow rather than being dissipated at the end of rows. Results from this technique are quite impressive, and show that, although less actual land is planted, crop yields per acre are significantly higher than those obtained by planting the same area in straight rows. This technique is very effective in ordinary vegetable gardens, by planting concentric rows of plants that are happy with one another. The genesic garden also includes a large 'crystal', a spherical structure made of metal tubing, based on the angles and proportions of the newly fertilised human ovum. These 'crystals' are usually about six feet in diameter and are placed at a particular energy centre related to the pattern of the various circles in the planting. This type of 'crystal' is outside the scope of this book, but there is an application of natural crystals to this sort of planting.

It has been suggested, and experiments are currently in progress, that certain types of natural crystals should be placed in the centre of each genesic circle. These circles are seldom more than a dozen feet in diameter, usually smaller; therefore, a relatively small crystal at the energy focus of each circle, particularly if it is programmed with the intention of aiding plant growth, could prove quite powerful. Once again, it will be necessary for the gardener to attune to various circles of plant growth, and to see which crystals are in harmony with that particular group of plants.

Once a crystal is programmed for a specific purpose, it is as well not to use it for other purposes. For example, if you are using a crystal for healing, it is better not to try to use that crystal for meditation or manifestation. In some instances, putting it to other uses will effectively cancel out the programme that you have put into it. If you *do* use a crystal that is already programmed for another purpose, be certain that you put the thought into the crystal before you use it and that it will *retain* the programme that is already been put into it.

An example of this is a London homoeopath who was using a crystal as a repository for homoeopathic informa-tion and intuition, which he used in combination with a crystal dowsing pendulum. He then decided to use his 'homoeopathic' crystal to help him reach higher spiritual levels in his own personal meditations. The crystal was quite helpful in this respect, and in effect took on the programming of this purpose, through the effect of picking up the intent of its use. In attempting to use the crystal in his homoeopathic work the next day, he found that his homoeopathic programming had been entirely erased!

You can see from this example that the use of crystals requires one other aspect of the user: *clarity of purpose*. You will find that, as you begin to use your crystals more and more, if you are not clear in your purpose before you begin, you probably will be by the time you are finished!

Crystals are often worn as amulets or talismans. Once again, the crystal is programmed for a specific intention. This was done a great deal in ancient times, of course, the programming of the particular piece being done through its carver. If we find an amulet dedicated to the goddess Astarte, then the person who made it would have been holding her image in his mind as he carved it, along with her associated attributes.

Another area in which crystals can prove very helpful falls not so much under the category of healing, but more under the category of 'preventive medicine'. This is in protection against psychic attack. There are various methods described in numerous books for dealing with psychic attack, but these are outside the scope of this book. Crystals, however, can be very effectively used as well as, or in conjuction with, other techniques.

In essence, you are using your crystal as a protective shield, and you will programme into your crystal whatever image is suggestive to you of protection. You might visualize this as a barrier of light surrounding your body; or you might even visualize it as a physical shield, bouncing back to the sender all negative energies that he has sent to you — or, even better, transmuting them into positive energies before returning them. There is no reason for not programming your crystal to act as a total protection against negative energies, whether directed at you or not. Why not visualize your protective field operating rather like the bow of a ship — just pushing aside and transmuting all negative energies that you might come into contact with. If you do use a crystal as a protective device you may wish either to wear it or carry it on your person, or perhaps in your handbag. Although you can will the crystal to generate its protective influence when you are at a distance from it, you should not expect its effect to be as powerful as it would be if it is on your person.

Likewise, you might wish to programme a crystal to protect your home or meditation area from negative energies. In fact, there is virtually no place or thing that cannot be protected in this way.

Crystals are also very effective as dowsing instruments. A natural crystal suspended from a chain (silver seems to be the most effective) is very useful as a 'yes-no' pendulum. You not only get the usual effect of the pendulum, but also the 'intention' response of the crystal. Another useful technique in dowsing is to hold a crystal in the hand opposite the pendulum, and use the pendulum in the normal manner. Persons using this technique have reported as much as a tenfold increase in the power of the pendulum.

One area of experimentation with crystals that has not been tried to any degree is using them as telepathic links. For this sort of usage one would need two crystals that are in harmony with each other, as well as telepathic ability in the users. Once again, the crystals are no substitute for natural ability: they merely add to it. The other possibility is to have two halves of the same crystal; that is, a crystal sawn in two. Should you choose to experiment in this way, you will need to find a lapidary who can do the sawing for you, as virtually any crystal you would use in such an **experiment would** be much harder than steel or glass and would need to be sawn using special equipment.

9.

Personal Healing

Healing is treated in this book as a separate subject, although it is obvious that the processes described in the previous chapter certainly involve healing in the spiritual sense. In this chapter we are concerned less with personal development than with physical healing.

The subject of healing is further divided for the purposes of discussion into *Personal Healing*, that is, the healing of the human body, and *Planetary Healing*, the healing of the Earth Body. In reality, of course, the two are inseparable: any wellness that is created *on* the Earth is wellness *for* the Earth. There is nothing in the chemical components of our physical bodies that does not come from the Earth, and that is, therefore, utterly and totally part of the planet. The crystal, as something which is part of and for the most part *is* the Earth body, becomes a direct physical link between the two. Biologists and chemists are beginning to discover that much of the matter which makes up the physical body is crystalline in nature, and even some of the liquid substances which make up the physical body have crystalline characteristics as discussed in a later chapter.

But the physical body is only one of several bodies which make up the total being. These other bodies are often referred to as the Subtle bodies and are principally composed of various levels and states of energy. Since crystals are also responsive to subtle energies (elemental energies, as discussed previously) the subtle bodies can also be treated through the use of crystals.

It is important to remember that healing does not *begin* in the physical body but in the subtle bodies, of which the physical body is only a reflection. And, since crystals are capable of dealing with energies from the lowest, such as electricity, to the highest, such as subtle spiritual energies, it becomes possible to treat a number of bodies simultaneously.

It is important that crystals are not 'taken like pills'. The nature of *healing*, as opposed to medicine, is the difference between *sensing* what a patient needs (through the intuition) and *thinking* about what the patient needs (the process of rational thought). The true healer, whether he or she uses crystals or not, principally operates through the intuitive link with the patient. Since the energies of the subtle bodies, like crystal energy, can only be sensed through intuition, it is only through such sensitivity that true healing using crystals take place.

Some illness however is caused by an outworking of the patient's karmic pattern, an outworking of what the patient has chosen to bring into this lifetime as physical illness. In such a case, the disease is not susceptible to healing by *any* method, and the patient is caused further distress by being given unnecessary hope. This is not to say, however, that they cannot be given love and understanding.

It is not necessary for the healer consciously to understand the laws of Karma, because the outworking of those laws is fully accessible to the intuition, the sensing mind. However, this does not mean that because the healer is not consciously aware of these laws he is not responsible for them. If we are going to treat illness on as many levels as we can reach (and aren't we, after all, only treating symptoms if we don't?), then we must make every effort to at least become intuitively aware of the rules that apply to each level. If we cannot be bothered to make the effort, then we probably have no business to attempt healing in the first place, because all we are doing is spreading more confusion through our own lack of spiritual integrity.

In our examination of the patient, the subtle body that will be the most apparent to the healer is the aura. This does not necessarily mean that the colours of the aura will be visible to the healer, but that at some level the healer will be able to sense the energies around the person, and in particular any areas of energy disharmony or disturbance indicative of disease.

The aura may be 'seen' psychically, or in some instances may be sensed by running the hand through it sensing areas of disturbance. If the patient has physical symptoms, then the areas of the body in which the physical symptoms occur would the natural places to begin looking for auric disturbances.

What exactly is the aura? The human body is principally an electrically operated instrument. Wherever electricity flows, such as in a wire, there is also an electrical field. The same is true with the human electrical field. This field is measurable, and since Kirlian photography was discovered we are now able to indirectly photograph this field. Scientific research has shown that the human body and sensory organs are extremely sensitive to various types of low level electrical and electro-magnetic energy, and it is this sensitivity which allows us to sense another person's electrical field, which is much of the energy we sense as the 'aura'. Certainly the aura contains the energies of all the subtle bodies, but it is these electrical emanations from the body that are the most 'visible'. We also know that any disturbance in the subtle bodies will reflect in the aura as a disturbance, and it is within this area of disturbance that we will discover symptoms occurring in the physical body.

There are several types of healing which take place in a healer-patient relationship. The most commonly used is *contact healing*, where the healer places his hands directly within the aura of the person, or often directly touches their physical body. With this type of healing, as with all other types, there is a transfer of energy from the healer to the patient. In *magnetic healing*, the healer transfers some of his own energy to the patient — a process often used by novice healers. As the healer grows in personal awareness, he will begin to realize that it is possible for him to become a channel for higher energies, and will begin to draw his healing energies from higher sources. In either case, however, the essence is energy transfer, causing a change in the auric and higher energies of the patient, which is ultimately reflected in the physical body.

Let us now think back to the chapter on the behaviour of energy within crystals. The most important discovery from that chapter was that crystals act as *transformers* and harmonizers of energy. Having realized that illness in the physical body is a reflection of disruption or disharmony of energies in the subtle bodies, and that healing takes place by restoring harmony to the subtle bodies, it becomes apparent that by merely placing the appropriate crystal in the area of energy disharmony (illness) and allowing its transformative power to work to bring the subtle energies back into harmony, healing will take place. And, in all of the bodies from subtle to physical.

Crystal healing takes place mainly in the subtle bodies. Crystal healing may be looked at as contact healing, that is, where the crystal is placed directly into the energy of the subtle bodies, or absent healing, where it is not. Absent healing may take place at any distance. Subtle energies are not susceptible to the limitations of time and space, so the distance at which absent healing takes place is not important.

In contact healing, the healer diagnoses the area of energy disturbance, and places the appropriate crystal into that area. In this instance, the crystal can be held by the healer, or by the patient, or perhaps even worn by the patient for a short period of time. Some common sense is necessary here, though. You are not likely to win converts for crystal healing if you have patients walking around for two weeks with a crystal tied to their head by a piece of purple ribbon — as one over-enthusiastic crystal healer did. In any case, the crystal serves as a focus of healing energy and healing intent, and therefore produces an appropriate energy. Even if no physical disease is present, the crystal can be used for cleansing and balancing the aura.

An alternative method is for both the patient and healer to hold crystals, although obviously the two crystals need to be in harmony with each other. One osteopath is trying an alternative to this method, using crystals that have been sawn in two: the patient and the healer then hold separate halves of the same crystal. A further alternative to this method is for the patient, or the patient and the healer, to hold crystals of different minerals in different hands. There is often an interaction between the crystals of various minerals and a balancing effect may be produced through the natural energies of the differing crystals. The actual minerals used will vary from patient to patient and can only be sensed by the healer, or by the reactions of the patient.

In healing with crystals, it does not seem to matter whether the crystal is in its natural state or whether has been shaped. Obviously sawing a crystal in two will change its properties somewhat, but as long as the crystals are properly cleansed to remove any trauma resulting from the cutting, they seem to work just as effectively. This also includes crystals which have been cut as gems.

The use of crystals in *chakra healing* and balancing is coming more and more into use. The techniques of contact and absent healing are equally applicable to the chakras, although the healer must be even more sensitive to his patient in this sort of healing, as considerable energy disturbance can be created if the wrong crystal or the wrong energy is used. Once again, it is up to the healer to experiment with various crystals and be sensitive to their effects. Many healers will discover that the crystals of certain minerals are more responsive to certain chakra energies than others. Recent experiments by the author have shown that placing crystals over various chakras causes a distinct reaction in brain wave patterns, particulary at a sub-conscious level. To produce effects at that level of energy, very strong reactions at higher levels must be taking place.

If a pendulum is being used for diagnosis it is found that a crystal pendulum is particularly responsive to chakra imbalances and often just the crystal of the pendulum is sufficient to achieve rebalancing. One practitioner using this method simply allows the crystal to swing freely in the chakra cone in either direction, using the intent of balance, until the swing stops. The chakra is then in balance.

As to which crystals are best for which chakras, there is no definite answer. Healers using colour for chakra healing will already know that there is no agreement on which colour to use. The same is true of crystals. Again the answer lies in the sensitivity of the healer to the patient's and the crystal's energies, and his ability to match the two in a given situation. Some healers have tried using a crystal similar in colour to the colours they have been using for chakra healing, but this is simply a point of departure.

Some healers are using one type of crystal, such as quartz, and then 'tuning' each crystal to a particular chakra. There is nothing really wrong with this, except that using only one mineral rather limits the range of crystal energies available. The chapter on workshop techniques will demonstrate how dramatically different these energies can be.

Crystals have a wide range of application when combined with acupressure and acupuncture techniques. There are several diagnostic techniques available to determine areas of weakness in the various lines of energy which flow through the body, but whatever method of diagnosis is being used, treatment with crystals will often show immediate results.

Crystals can be held in the hand while acupressure is being applied, or they can be directly applied to the acupressure points in place of finger contact. If you are going to use this technique, though, it is recommended that the point of the crystal be rounded off with sandpaper, as the sharp point is likely to puncture the skin. Remember to cleanse the crystal of the shock of grinding its point.

In acupuncture a crystal can be used in contact with the needle, or be held in the hand as the needle is placed into the body.

Harry Oldfield, a London practitioner, has invented a device consisting of a white sound frequency generator connected to a hollow glass tube filled with various crystals and a saline solution. The white sound is translated into an electric current, which passes through the tube (called a 'wand'), stimulating the crystals.

The wand is then placed against the body, usually at an

acupressure or acupuncture point. There seems to be a response between the wand and the body's physical makeup, especially bone tissue. Results in treating a wide range of complaints have been good.

There are numerous injuries and illnesses that can potentially be treated with crystal energies. Little has been done in most of these areas, however, and it is suggested that crystal healing be added to other techniques that are already in use.

We should not reject out of hand so-called orthodox medicine, as there is much that alternative medicine cannot heal that is perfectly within the realm of orthodox techniques. There are few alternative medicine practioners that would be qualified to rebuild a shattered leg bone, as an example. Let us look at some areas now mostly in the domain of orthodox treatment and see how crystals might supplement such treatment.

The treatment of many types of emotional illness might be effectively supplemented with crystals. Certain crystals, such as those of aquamarine, and occasionally tourmaline, produce a calming effect in many people, and probably induce subtle changes in brain wave patterns. Certainly treatment with crystals in conjunction with ordinary methods of psychoanalysis, or other treatments of mental disturbance, could be quite effective.

A by-product of our technological age is the production of all sorts of electro-magnetic waves of many different wavelengths. Many of these can be disruptive to brain-waves, and the use of crystals could help to re-establish normal brainwave patterns in people who develop anxiety symptoms as a result of these artificially generated waves.

Other types of brain-related illness such as epilepsy and strokes may also prove to be susceptible to crystal healing, although it is not known whether any techniques have been developed along these lines. Certainly the grounding effect of crystals could be very useful in the treatment of epilepsy, because in an epileptic seizure the subtle bodies often become misaligned or completely separated from the physical body.

We find that information transfer in the brain probably takes place through liquid crystals. Thus, illnesses of the mind, or of the physical brain, should be very susceptible to crystal healing because there is harmony between the crystals of an organic nature (the brain) and the crystals of inorganic nature, such as are used in healing. Thus, it is not unlikely that we will find it possible to begin healing damaged brain tissue, or at least reprogramming undiseased brain tissue to take over the function of the damaged areas. In this type of healing, the crystal would be programmed with the intention of reprogramming the brain cells, and then applied directly to the head in whatever location feels best to the patient. This could be particularly useful in treating diseases such as alcoholism, which have a long-term degenerative effect on brain tissue.

In the treatment of the internal organs, we cannot implant a crystal into the organ, or have access to it, other than access to its disturbance of the body's energy field. Australian Aborigines do actually implant crystals, but it appears that they are inserted only under the skin.

In most cases of healing diseased organs, the crystal is held or placed into the area of disturbed energy on the outside of the body; as the energy field reharmonises, so does the diseased organ. There is no specific rule as to the exact distance the crystal is held from the body or the direction in which it is pointed. The patient must try various distances and orientations of the crystal for himself until he feels an appropriate response. The exact response may be a lessening of pain or discomfort, a fluttering feeling around the diseased area, heat, cold, or simply a feeling of well-being. As always the best clue is always what feels 'right'.

Certain types of injuries to the body, particularly those involving the bone structure, tend to cause disturbances of the body's energy field that last longer than certain other types of injuries, such as those to the skin or muscles. This is due to the crystalline nature of the bones themselves, and the fact that pain or injury tends to 'programme' itself into the bone structure as it occurs. This is also true in the case of arthritis, which can be the crystalline material of the joint surfaces beginning to degenerate. In either case, what is important is that the bone material itself is programmed, so treatment with crystals becomes more a matter of *de*-programming. In this instance, you would programme your crystal with the intention of extracting from the bone tissue its unharmonious programming, and drawing that disharmony into the crystal itself. The same applies with broken bones. In all of these instances, you will probably find certain positions of the crystal that will feel better than others, and if applied immediately after an injury has been treated by ordinary medical means, such as setting the bone, there may be a lessening of pain in certain directions. Obviously, if you have pulled a negative programme from the bone into your crystal, it will be necessary to cleanse the crystal immediately after use.

It is especially important that, when using a crystal to relieve the trauma programmed into broken bones, you leave in the bone the programme that deals with the re-knitting of the bone tissue, or even reinforce it.

For cuts and other types of wounds where the skin is punctured, once appropriate measures have been taken to stop the bleeding, it may be found that crystals can be helpful in reducing shock, and in beginning immediate regeneration of the injured tissues. Normally the crystal is placed in proximity to the wound and the patient is asked to breath deeply. This will help to lessen the effects of shock, since the crystal works in the subtle bodies where the symptons of shock manifest themselves most. There is also a reduction in pain and the crystal will act as a link between both sides of the wound, so that the programming of the subtle bodies to begin healing can take place at once. Once again, the positioning of the crystal is important, and it may be necessary to move the crystal in various directions until an effect is felt. If no effect is felt by the patient, then just use the crystal in any orientation that feels comfortable to the user.

Apply this same technique after surgery, but apply the healing from the deepest levels outward. In this case, you should intend supplementing the body's own natural healing programme, rather than try to impose one of your own. But *do* use the crystal to draw the trauma of the operation from the tissue, as the trauma often blocks the natural healing process. If the patient has used a crystal for meditation, by all means have them use it at this time in a meditative state to help realign the subtle bodies, which are often badly out of line due to the effects of anaesthetics. Rebalancing the energy of the chakras is particularly useful at this point.

Remember that when you are using crystals for healing of any type, they must be cleaned and recleaned constantly, as you are often pulling the body's programming of the disease or injury into the crystal.

One other crystal healing method that should be mentioned here is one that is particularly in use in the East. Often crystals are crushed to a powder and taken internally. *Under no circumstances should you do this!* Remember, the power of the crystal is the result of its internal form: by destroying that form, you destroy the most beneficial effects. Besides, some crystals can be poisonous.

In absent healing, either by individuals or by groups, the use of a crystal as a focus of will and intention is particularly powerful. In this instance, especially, we are enlisting the aid of the elemental of crystals to act as a 'telephone line' for the energies to be sent. The crystals in use in this situation are often described as transmitters of energy, but that term is rather misleading. A radio transmitter, for instance, broadcasts powerful electromagnetic waves (radio waves), whereas a crystal merely 'clears the way' so that healing energies can be sent with the minimum of outside interference.

Again, the crystals supplement whatever technique the healer is already using. If colour is being used, then send it through the crystal. If visualization is used, try visualizing the person inside the crystal with all of its harmonizing influences. Just holding the crystal while healing is sent is also effective. One healer has had good results by using a photograph of the patient, and placing the crystal on top of it with the appropriate intention.

Healers who use crystals often report a pulsing of energy from the crystals as they are used. From our chapter on the atom, we remember that as energy moves about in the atom from level to level, it does not wander aimlessly but jumps in very definite leaps from step to step inside the atom. This pulsing suggests that this is taking place inside the crystal as healing energies are drawn through it. In other words, the crystal momentarily accumulates energy until it can release it in a quantum burst.

The various healing techniques described in this section are by no means all-inclusive, and are merely presented to serve as a guide line. Every healer will develop his or her own techniques, and there are an infinite number of combinations and variations.

Self-healing

The question of choosing the proper crystal for self-healing is more difficult, because the person seeking healing may not have a particularly well developed intuition, nor be inclined to believe it if he does. Nonetheless, it is preferable in almost all instances for the patient to choose his or her own crystal. It is desirable to have a good selection of crystals available, preferably of several minerals. This allows the patient to select the individual crystal which is in greatest harmony with their own particular energy. The question may well arise that, if you are choosing a crystal in harmony with your own energy, will that crystal necessarily harmonize the energies of illness? The intuition is used in this selection process, the intuition being an aspect of our higher being, which always knows our needs.

This still does not solve the problem of the person who is unaware of or indifferent to his intuitive powers. There are several techniques for reaching the intuitive powers. As previously mentioned, almost all of us have had the experience of 'first impressions' — that feeling you get on meeting a new person or a new situation, that you often try to talk yourself out of later on, but that always proves correct in the end. This method is particularly usable in selecting crystals.

There are several ways to apply this technique. The first, is simply to shut your eyes, relax for a second or two, then open your eyes suddenly and literally grab the first crystal that comes into your awareness. If there are several, set them apart and use the method again on this group. Another method is to choose a number of crystals that you are drawn to, for whatever reason, and then, once again, use the same method.

It is often enough simply to reach into a box of crystals with the eyes closed and take out whatever crystal the hand is led to. There is certainly nothing wrong with using this method with the eyes open, but it is often tempting to choose the 'prettier' one that is next to the one that you *really* felt drawn to. You will notice that in each of these methods, there is that element of 'first impression', that is, making your choice before you actually have a chance to *think* about what you are doing.

If you are choosing your crystals from someone who works with them esoterically, then there is certainly nothing wrong with allowing them to aid you in your choice. You could ask them to pick out a dozen or so crystals which their intuition suggests might be helpful, and then make your final choice from those — keeping in mind once again that the final choice is always yours, and that even though they have chosen a certain group of crystals, it could still be that *none* of their choices are the right one.

For those who trust their intuition the choice of a particular crystal becomes very much easier, and all that is necessary is to find someone or some place where there is a large selection of crystals.

The guidance as to the particular type of crystal needed may come totally through intuition in the moment, or it may be received in a meditation, or perhaps even from a Spirit Guide if you have reached such a level of contact. The final choice, however, should always be the user's. There are numerous advertisements in various esoteric magazines offering crystals for various purposes, and plenty of people are offering to choose them for others. Ignore them. Remember that it is worse to have the *wrong* crystal, than no crystal at all!

The results obtained from various types of healing techniques are often quite subjective, and although they have worked for some people it does not follow that they will work for everyone. Moreover, the laws of karma still apply no matter what the healing situation, and there will be negative results if these laws have not been satisfied.

It is desirable to heal in the highest subtle bodies, but the person performing self-healing may not necessarily have any sensitivity whatever to disturbance in these bodies — at least not directly. But if the patient has chosen his crystal intuitively, and with the intention of self-healing, he will have been drawn as nearly as possible to the correct one.

The actual techniques are easy enough — placing the crystal in the aura either by wearing it, holding it in the hand and passing it through the aura, or perhaps even placing it under the pillow or bed during sleep. Again it is a matter of whatever feels right to the patient and it must be strongly emphasized that the techniques of crystal healing are not meant to replace, but rather to supplement, other types of treatment, such as homoeopathy, acupuncture or, in some instances, standard medical practice.

The techniques discussed in treatment of the brain and in mental illness can also be used in self-healing, but the actual programming of the crystals used by the patient might be best done by a healer, or by a disinterested party. Obviously if the patient has some degree of mental disturbance, it may be difficult for him to undertake clear programming of the crystal for the self-healing process. It is also necessary that the patient use common sense, recognizing that if he continues to fill his body with caffeine, sugar and other unhealthy substances, then all healing techniques are ultimately doomed to fail.

10.

Planetary Healing

The Earth is part of a greater universal pattern, beginning with the solar system and extending outwards to the galaxy itself. Anything that happens on the Earth will create ripples far beyond the immediate vicinity of the planet. Thus the question of planetary healing has even wider implications than just the Earth itself.

But how did the Earth get to its current state? Many, many people are beginning to have memories of past time on the Earth (including the writer), memories which correspond in relevant details, memories by people who are often quite unaquainted, and even living continents apart.

In the age of the Earth known as the Atlantean, the Earth was beginning to reach fulfilment as a place where the consciousness of man was implanting the essence of spirit in the dense matter of the Earth — the purpose for which the race of man was created. But, as man became more *self*-conscious, he began to separate his own wants and desires from the needs of the Spirit from which he was created.

Crystals were widely used in Atlantis as part of this work, drawing their power and energy through the universal elemental (or deva) of crystals. But it is important to remember that this was a two-way exchange. As men on the Earth consciously began to bring spirit into matter through crystal power, every crystal in the universe responded through the elemental of crystals, taking into their programming the higher energies the race of man was using through them. We begin to see why working consciously with crystals on a planetary basis not only affects the planet, but the entire Cosmos, and why when those powers are misused or misdirected the ripples of disharmony spread far beyond the planet. This was what happened in Atlantis and was the reason for the destruction of the Atlantean civilization.

There were crystals of all sorts in use in Atlantis, ranging from huge crystals several feet across in the major temples, to smaller, hand-sized crystals for use in healing disease. Synthetic crystals were also used, mostly created toward the end of Atlantis in forms and with energies far removed from the harmonies and universal attunement of the elemental. The largest crystals were either located on, or linked to, major points of Earth power. These points are at the crossing of lines of Earth energy, and are comparable to acupuncture points on the human body. These lines would have been part natural and part artificial with the Atlanteans reinforcing certain lines with their crystals through conscious effort.

At some point some of the priesthood in charge of the major crystals began to make decisions in their own interests rather than in the interests of the planet, and that is where it all began to go wrong. The power of crystals is neither good or evil — it just exists. Like any other spiritual tool, the good to which it is put is entirely dependent upon the will and consciousness of the user. Finally there came a point at which the Atlanteans attempted to restructure the surface of the Earth itself — they were, in fact, trying to move continents! And with the power that was available through the major crystals, this was entirely feasible.

It was then that the Heirarchy that oversees the development of the Earth decided that it must step in and intervene to prevent this happening. Such use of crystals definitely contravened all laws governing such power, and went not only directly against the best interests of the Earth, but of the solar system itself. Messages were sent to the unafflicted priesthood, and there was virtually an overnight migration from the islands and continents that made up Atlantis. These few priests made their way to various parts of the world that were still developing (even as we see various levels of development on the Earth today), where they carried the inner spiritual knowledge and established themselves among native populations where possible. Such were the roots of the earliest civilizations of Tibet, Mesopotamia, China, and Egypt, and others that did not survive and mature.

But almost before the enlightened priesthood had left, agencies from outside the Earth had removed the major crystals; but since so much of the Earth's own energy system was linked in to them, and because by this time there was a great deal of stress and disharmony in the linking energies, their removal caused cataclysmic changes to take place. The most immediate effect was the break-up and disintegration of the various Atlantean landmasses where the crystals were situated. There would have been major earthquakes, and land masses either rising or subsiding. There would have been global weather changes. One can easily imagine that the flood stories of Noah and of Gilgamesh would have originated at this time. We could liken this period of Earth history to surgery on a human body. A great deal of pain and trauma, followed by a long period of healing and recuperation.

The laws of Karma work on a planetary as well as a personal basis. In fact, it might be said that the karma of the Earth is the collective karma of the race of man. And in this particular case, it was considerable.

Karma can be thought of as a balance of energy — if you produce x amount of negative or disharmonious energy, then you must produce x amount of positive energy to compensate. Or even better, take the negative energy back into yourself and transmute it to positive.

This is just what the race of man has been doing since Atlantis. We have been taking back into ourselves the negative energy sent out into the universe in Atlantis, bringing that energy into form through hatred and violence and dissipating it. If you are angry and hold it

inside, the energy remains, but if you bring it into form by
striking a punch bag (or the person who made you angry)
the energy of anger is transmuted into mechanical energy
and dissipated. When the energy of anger has been
balanced by the mechanical energy of striking, or even
vocalizing (vibration of air), the energy is gone. The scales
balance.

If this sounds a little severe, it is well to remember a few
things. First, that a very large proportion of the souls on
the Earth at any given time through history have been the
very same souls that were present in Atlantis — who
contributed through their own lack of spiritual integrity to
its downfall. Secondly, that the soul is utterly
indestructible, and although the physical body may die,
the soul collects another body at a later time and comes
back to continue transmuting.

If we keep in mind that the Earth is a school, a place of
learning, then all the various 'misfortunes' that seem to
befall mankind may be seen as learning experiences. And
lastly, but perhaps most important, that since the soul is
indestructible, it is also timeless; the 12,000 years or so
since Atlantis fell is therefore a relatively short period, and
is really of minor consequence to souls which are perhaps
millions of years old.

The time which we are just entering on the Earth, which
is being called the New Age, is the time of completion of
planetary karma, and it is time to once again take up our
spiritual mantle, both individually and as a planet.

At this moment on the Earth many New Age centres are
being founded, and some have been in operation for many
years. It is in certain of these centres that major crystals are
now being used, crystals which will serve the same positive
uses as the major Atlantean crystals, but, one hopes, with a
higher degree of consciousness.

These centres are located at major crossing points of the
Earth's energy grid, both the natural grid and the remains
of the Atlantean system. It is from these various centres
that a conscious restructuring of planetary energies will
take place, and through these centres that much of the
energy of the New Age is being and will be fed into the
Earth. But before we take a further look at the Earth's

future, let's look once more into the past.

As the preceding few paragraphs show, one of the major works that has been and will once again be undertaken with crystals, is to work directly with the energies on the planet. Man has attempted to tap back into these planetary energy sources at numerous times since the fall of Atlantis, and the Earth is littered with artefacts resulting from these attempts. One of the earliest was the Great Pyramid of Giza. There has probably been more mystical nonsense written about this structure than about any other structure in the history of the planet. The pyramid shape certainly has unique energy properties — particularly the ability to alter time/space. It is these qualities of timelessness and spacelessness that make such a structure compatible with crystals, since the ability to use crystals without the usual limitations of time and space increases their power. It was no accident that the Great Pyramid was built in the exact shape of the Golden Temple of Atlantis. The Great Pyramid is an artefact of a time when the Egyptian priesthood felt themselves sufficiently re-evolved spiritually to attempt reconstructing the Atlantean civilization. It was this ability of the pyramid to alter time/space which suggested to later Egyptian cultures, with their particular emphasis on the preservation of the physical body, their suitability as tombs — though this was the one thing they were *never* intended to be.

There are a great many erroneous conclusions drawn in various current publications concerning the mineralogy of the various stones used in the Great Pyramid. Particular emphasis is placed on the fact that the King's Chamber and certain inner structures are made of granite, a rock high in quartz content. Vast calculations are made, purporting to show the incredible electrical capacity of that volume of quartz being subjected to the pressures inside the Great Pyramid, but with a complete misunderstanding of how energies behave in crystals. These misunderstandings are examined in the next chapter.

But what can happen, and frequently does, in these megalithic structures is that the stone from which they are constructed does have an energy altering effect on the natural Earth energies which flow through them. In this case, there is a constant flow of energy from the Earth, and therefore a constant alteration of that energy by the minerals making up the stones. This effect was clearly known to the ancients, probably more through sensitivity and intuition than through conscious knowledge, and it was utilized to great effect in almost all ancient structures, including the Great Pyramid. The Great Pyramid is located at a particular crossing of Earth energy lines (called ley lines) and therefore becomes a major accumulator and modifier of energy. These same energy-altering properties can also be seen in many of the other ancient structures of Egypt, especially in the earliest constructions at Thebes (modern Luxor) and other of the oldest temple sites.

Another classic example of this type of sensitive construction took place at Stonehenge in Britain, though at a much later time. The stones for the construction of Stonehenge were transported great distances and are in particular mineralogical harmony with the earth energies at the site. Not only that, but stones of different types (and therefore mineralogically different) were used in different parts of Stonehenge, thus creating an energy flow and localized areas of energy accumulation within the structure. It was these localized energy accumulations that the priesthood were tapping for their various rituals, and for their abilities to steer their communities intuitively.

Other stone structures, such as the pyramids in Mexico and Central America, many of the megalithic structures in South America, and the construction of 'medicine wheels' in North America, all seem to be reflections of this same attunement to earth energy flow. Remember that it is only recently that large segments of mankind have not lived close to the land and have begun to lose this attunement to Earth energies. We have by no means lost this feeling entirely, though, for many readers will have had the experience of travelling from place to place and feeling very comfortable and 'at home' in some places, and totally uncomfortable in others. In many instances this will be a reflection of the traveller's attunement to the Earth energies in the various places, which in turn will be largely dependent on the mineral make-up of the particular location. As a brief example of this, areas of granite rock which make up many of the Earth's major mountain chains produce high amounts of natural radioactivity, which in turn produces more negative ionization of the air around them. Recent studies have shown that people generally feel mentally clearer and more alert the more negative ions are in the air. Perhaps this is the reason that mystics have traditionally been found on mountain tops!

There is one other aspect of crystal energies which must be mentioned before returning to the current planetary picture regarding crystals. This might be called *crystal power*. Crystal power is an energy that responds solely through crystals, and is an extension of the powers of the elemental of crystals. Crystal power was withdrawn mostly from the Earth at the same time as the Atlantean crystals, and only remained in the smallest amounts through the building of the Great Pyramid. The other aspect of the building of the Great Pyramid was to act as a Great Crystal, as an accumulator for the small amounts of crystal power remaining on the earth at that time. With the failure of the Egyptian priesthood to use even these small powers correctly, the final remnants of crystal power were withdrawn approximately five thousand years ago.

So then, the other aspect of the New Age is that not only has the Earth completed its planetary karma, but much of the power available to the Atlanteans for planetary work, and indeed work beyond the planet, will also be returned. With the return of powerful crystals to New Age temple centres, a process which has already begun, crystal power is even now beginning to trickle back into Earth's energy structure, a process which will accelerate rapidly over the next few years. It will be the work of those in such centres to control and direct this energy properly as it comes back into the Earth's energy grid, and also to protect it against misuse. As more crystal power is fed into the Earth's body, individual crystals will also become much more powerful, requiring higher and higher degrees of awareness from their users.

We are now in what we might call a 'training period' for the time when sufficient crystal power will come into the Earth to be dangerous if used incorrectly. All of those who are being drawn to work with crystals today are truly hearing the call of the planet, and the call of the cosmos to once again begin to understand this energy, and to use it properly. This book is a direct outgrowth of that call, and those who are drawn to read it will be responding to the same call. Most of those who are drawn to work with crystals have used them before, some correctly, and some incorrectly. Crystals were certainly used in many cultures and civilizations after the time of Atlantis, and there were equal opportunities in those civilizations for proper use or misuse. Once again let us remind ourselves that although we have been speaking of Atlanteans as someone else, *we are* the Atlanteans. So, fellow Atlanteans, how is it going to go *this* time?

Another of the major works to be undertaken by the New Age crystal centres is that of consciously working to rebalance and reharmonize planetary energies. The ley line system is in a poor state and will take a great deal of straightening out; but this needs to be done with total awareness of the needs of the planet. As other New Age centres grow in strength, there will also be continuous adjustments to be made in the energy structure, and in some instances, entirely new ley lines will be forged.

It is necessary here to mention also the Earth changes that are being forecast by many seers. Many involve land mass changes, some of which would be as dramatic as the Earth's readjustment during Atlantean times. One thing that must be emphasized is that these changes are the last resort of the planet, and will occur only if man is unable to make the proper planetary adjustments himself. We can be assured that these changes will take place only in the last second of the 11th hour, and will only take place in proportion to what man has not done himself for the planet. In either case, the needs of the planet will be fulfilled, but it will certainly be a great deal more comfortable for us if we can relieve the planet of the necessity to create its own adjustments! Should it be necessary for the planet to readjust itself, however, then obviously the palnetary network will need constant re-adjustment and rebalancing, and this will also be a role undertaken by the crystal centres, should it be necessary.

Although this chapter has been entitled Planetary Healing, the word healing has hardly been mentioned; yet can we not see that in healing the Earth Body the situation is exactly the same as in healing the human body — that is, to bring the energies of the body back into harmony with the Universal Flow. This process of deliberately rebalancing planetary energies will have much the same effect as chakra balancing in the human body: as these energies are reharmonized, healing will follow automatically. As we change the very energy structure of the Earth itself, anything built upon the Earth that is not part of the new structure and the new energies will automatically fall away, since its foundations no longer have roots. Thus, the Old Age will fall away not by frontal assault, but by undermining its energy foundations.

What exactly is the role of the individual crystal user in all this? Not everyone will be drawn to one of the crystal centres, nor will many of you wish to be. Truly, it does not matter. The harmonizing effect of all this new energy and power flowing into the Earth will be available to everyone who can attune to it, and each and every person who can will become a part of the largest crystal centre — the Earth itself.

So the individual crystal user, as he goes about his daily work, whatever that may be, will create whatever wellness and harmony he can within his own reach, and wherever he creates wellness, it is a net gain to the planet. Every person, every plant, every animal that we heal is part of the Earth Being, and every morsel of food or drop of water or breath of air that we bless creates more and more wellness for the Earth.

If you wish to heal the Earth Body directly, then use whatever crystal healing techniques you are already using, and heal the Earth Body as you would a person's physical body. You probably won't have far to look for areas of disharmony to work on.

The important thing about crystals is that they are rather like the fulcrum of a lever: when they are placed in the right place at the right time, their effect is out of all proportion to their size. An ancient Greek once said: 'Give me a long enough lever and a place to stand, and I will move the Earth.' What he didn't say is that the fulcrum of that lever need have been no larger than a pea! A clear example of this sort of power was given to the writer during a recent visit to Egypt, when he was asked by his spirit teachers to place a small, specially shaped crystal at a particular point of power in one of the old Egyptian temples. Having managed to do so, on leaving the temple he was worried about it being found and removed, and asked the question of his guides, 'How long does it have to be in place?'

The reply came back, 'How long does it take a match to start a forest fire'

11.

Some Misconceptions

There are several other types of 'crystals' that should be mentioned, some of which will be useful to the user of crystals, and some which will not.

The first type is not a crystal at all, but merely carries the name. This is crystal glass, also called leaded glass. This name is applied to a particular type of glass, usually high in lead content, that is often used in stemware, vases, etc. It is also frequently cut into various many-faceted forms, such as bowls, candlesticks, and even into drops for chandeliers and so forth. It must be emphasized that, in all of its forms, it is a *glass*. By its very definition, a glass is a substance that has *no* regular internal structure — rather like a solidified jelly. And since it has no regular structure, it possesses none of the energy changing properties of natural crystals. Crystal glass is unusable in the same sense in which natural crystals are used.

Liquid crystals are similarly of little immediate importance to the crystal user. These are semi-solids in which the molecules of the liquid are arranged in regular patterns. Many types of living tissue are composed of liquid crystal, and it is thought that much of the memory storing capacity of the brain is made up of liquid crystals. These crystals are generally microscopic in size, and although of great importance generally, are of little use specifically in the terms in which we have been speaking of crystal usage.

Many different types of crystals are grown artificially, and most of these take on the same forms and mundane energy characteristics of natural crystals. The aspect of these which makes them generally unusable, however, is that at a subtle level, the crystal takes on a great deal of the energy of its growth environment. The growing environment of an artificial crystal is very clinical and sterile and far removed from any sort of natural environment.

Many of these crystals are being grown from materials, and in forms, that are not found naturally and which therefore violate the laws of natural matter. In other words, we have 'forced' these crystals to grow against their own nature. Obviously, crystals grown in such environments are not likely to harmonize well with natural energies, and in particular crystals which are forcefully grown are most unlikely to be in harmony with the energies of the elemental of crystals.

Several types of crystals are regularly grown in the laboratory, including quartz crystals for the electronics industry, ruby crystals for lasers, sapphires for bearings and substitute gems, emeralds for gems, diamonds for industrial use, rutile as a diamond substitute, and garnet as a diamond substitute. In the latter case, the garnet grown is yttrium-aluminium garnet, which does not occur in nature. It is colourless, has a high refractive index and is one of the 'forced' crystals that was mentioned earlier. Crystals of silicon metal are also grown and are the so-called 'silicon chips' that are used in computers. These crystals do not occur naturally either, and are often a source of confusion to many of the uninformed writing about the esoteric properties of minerals, since they are often confused with quartz, which is silicon dioxide and which has none of the peculiar electrical properties of the pure metal silicon. At the time of writing, the Soviet Union has just successfully grown silicon crystals in an orbiting laboratory, in zero gravity conditions, which allows extremely pure crystals to form — if one can consider such forced growth as pure.

This is not to suggest that laboratory-grown crystals are totally without use, however, as crystals that are grown in agreement with and in harmony with the elemental of crystals can be grown for very special purposes. As we know, a crystal incorporates much of the energy of its growing environment into its form; so imagine, if you will, a quartz crystal grown with a group of people continually directing pure love into it as it grows! Or for that matter, a group of people directing pure Christ energy into a crystal through its growing process. The implications of this are enormous, and as yet largely unexplored. Chapter 13 shows how you can grow certain types of crystals yourself, in your own home. Why not try growing a few crystals under such an environment, and, see what happens? It will obviously take some degree of commitment, because it takes several weeks to grow a crystal an inch or more in diameter; but it would also be possible to grow such crystal in the presence of natural crystals that have been programmed to 'feed it' with energies as it grows.

So far, the crystals we have been discussing are all made of so-called solid matter; but there is one other type of crystal which is not made of matter at all. Think for a moment what constitutes a crystal in the first place. It is a group of atoms arranged in a regular and repetitive pattern, held in rigid position by the atomic forces acting between each individual atom. But what is an atom? We have discovered in previous chapters that the atom is mostly empty space, held together by energy; and the minute particles which make up the atom seem to be composed of nothing but pure energy in themselves. So what is a crystal then, but energy held in rigid space by more energy! If, therefore, we are going to deal with objects that are composed of nothing but energy in the first place, why not dispense with the matter state altogether, and use nothing but pure energy?

This is just what mankind has been doing for thousands of years, except we have forgotten what it is that we are actually building. And the means by which we build these crystals of energy is called ritual. This is really all that happens in performing various sorts of rituals, building an energy form, a form which, by its repetitive and purpose-built nature, becomes an energy crystal. But with this realization, and our own improved inner awareness, it is possible to begin building such crystals of energy by working directly with the energies and seeing through the intuitive sense what it is we are building, rather than just the mindless repetition of some ritual. In other words, dispense with the ritual altogether, and simply *work with the energies*.

Things Crystals Are Not

It would be possible to write an entire book (and many people have unwittingly done so) based on misconceptions about crystals. Most of the writers of these books are very well-intentioned, often quite articulate, but, regretfully, badly misinformed about the most basic properties of crystals.

The first, and probably most misunderstood property of crystals, is the piezoelectric effect. As discussed in a previous chapter, this effect is produced by the stripping of the electrons from the outer atomic shells when a crystal is subjected to stress. This effect is most commonly misunderstood: the crystal is pictured as some sort of sponge into which vast quantities of electricity may be poured and stored and then squeezed out for use at some future time.

Once we understand the balance of energies that takes place within a crystal, we realize the utter impossibility of such a picture: a crystal gives off in another form exactly the amount of energy that is put in, and at virtually the same instant.

Nor do crystals store light; nor do naturally occurring crystals convert light to electricity — a misunderstanding of the artificially grown crystals of silicon metal, which do not occur in nature and which seem to be frequently confused with quartz (quartz being made of silicon and oxygen).

Another area of misunderstanding, in relation to quartz crystals in particular, is the role that they play in electronics. The fact that they are used in radio transmitters and receivers and in amplifiers does not mean that they *are* amplifiers, transmitters, etc. As discussed in Chapter 7, if electricity is put into slices of quartz crystals cut in certain crystal orientations, then the crystal will vibrate at a certain frequency. It is this ability to control vibrational frequency that is made use of in electronics. But that is *all* that they are used for, and only make up a small part of the mechanism of the transmitter or amplifier. Thus, we are not likely to look backward in history and find cavemen, or Egyptian priests for that matter, sending one another radio messages on quartz crystals. Some writers seem to believe that you only have to stick a crystal in your ear and dial Peru! This is not to say that they may not be useful as telepathic devices, as discussed in Chapter VII; but in no sense is the crystal actually doing the transmitting.

Several publications have taken the view that the Earth itself is a crystal, based on the geometric form of an icosahedron combined with a dodecahedron. Various purported positions of the intersection of faces and crystal edges are drawn on the Earth's surface, and then these various positions are studied to try to find archaeological evidence of particular activity along these lines.

Unfortunately for this theory, the Earth is predominantly covered with water and many of these lines and points tend to fall in and across various oceans. The various archaeological artefacts that are described as forming concentrations around certain points often cover as much as three to four hundred square miles on the ground surface. Not only that, the most fundamental aspects of crystals are completely ignored — that they have precise internal arrangement, and precise external symmetry. A quick glance at a globe, or a map of the Earth, will soon inform the reader of exactly how symmetrical the Earth is! Even if we were to use other criteria, such as the size, shape, and distribution of continental plates, we would find once again that the Earth is anything but symmetrical.

Having mentioned some of the basic misunderstandings about crystals, we should now look at some of the conclusions that have been drawn from these misconceptions.

A direct outgrowth of the various misunderstandings about the behaviour of quartz crystals under compression leads to a whole further series of misunderstandings about how quartz-bearing rocks behave under compression. The example usually seen in most articles is the rock granite, which in some instances may contain up to 50% quartz. It is assumed that since quartz crystals give off a momentary electrical charge when they are rapidly compressed, then the quartz grains in granite must do the same. This ignores two very important factors. The first is that the energy properties of single crystals are highly directional in nature, and if forces are applied other than in very specific directions, nothing happens. Secondly, and most important, the quartz crystals in granite are not well-formed; they are orientated almost at random, that is, the crystallizing axes point in virtually all directions. In a piece of granite used in building construction, such as in the King's Chamber and roof supports in the Great Pyramid, the compressive forces are highly directional and relate to the amount of stone that is piled on top of them. It would be very surprising indeed if even 1 per cent of the quartz grains in granite (and remember these are not *crystals*) were aligned closely enough to the compressive direction to have any chance whatever of producing an electrical charge. And, once the compression stabilizes, there is no further energy that *can* be given off. Once the energies have balanced (when the last block was put on the pyramid), nothing further happens.

In various articles, the positioning of the ceiling blocks in the Great Pyramid are described as capacitors or rectifiers and were supposedly connected to copper wires or rods to the outside of the Pyramid. Regretfully, there is no archaeological evidence of this whatever.

Another point worth making about quartz-bearing rocks such as granite, is that they are often seen as blocks of building material separated from their natural environment; many writers propose energy properties that relate directly to the amount of stone that is piled on top of them. If such rocks do possess such incredible energy properties then why are we not looking at them in terms of the place where the *greatest* compressive load is being applied to them — the mountains themselves! In this instance, rather than perhaps a hundred feet or so of rock piled on top of the granite blocks in a pyramid, we sometimes have *thousands* of feet of rock piled on top of granite. According to the logic of these writers, in this situation the quartz-bearing rocks should be producing bolts of electricity like a power station! Geological studies have shown that this is not the case, and although there are definite changes in magnetic fields and gravity fields around different types of rock, the changes are so subtle that it takes extremely sensitive instruments to measure them.

To be sure, the construction materials inside the Great Pyramid were very carefully chosen, but not for their ability to generate vast amounts of electrical energy. The Pyramid shape itself has very remarkable energy properties, but it deals with subtle energies, rather than the mundane energies of mechanics and electricity.

As for stone circles, the stones from which these were made were very carefully selected for their overall properties, and they definitely cause localized disturbances or accumulations of various types of energy. But once again, many writers are insisting on attributing these effects to piezoelectricity, which in many instances they are attributing to underground water flows affecting the roots of the stones. This encompasses two areas of massive misunderstanding — the nature of underground water flow in the first instance, and the nature of the hydrostatic effect (water pressure) in the second.

Such writers seem to be assuming that underground water flow takes the nature of rivers or streams on the surface — that there are large volumes of water presumably flowing through cavities in the rocks below. Although this does happen on very rare occasions in cave systems, the likelihood of it ever happening anywhere near a stone circle, and particularly where the roots of the stones would protude into the water flow, is almost non-existent. Almost all rocks are slightly porous, that is, they are rather like a sponge, in that they have minute air spaces between the various particles that make up the stone. These pore spaces are the largest in sedimentary rocks, a typical example of which would be sandstone. Flow also takes place in sands and gravels that have not yet been consolidated into rock. But porous space in these rocks seldom exceeds 10 to 15 per cent of the total volume, and the pore spaces themselves are rarely as large as half the size of a pinhead. Thus in underground water flow, we are not talking about a vast torrent but a slow oozing of water from one pore space to the next. Even in the relatively porous gravels of unconsolidated material, the rate of flow seldom exceeds a few feet per day. Hardly a raging torrent! Nor do such underground flows take on the characteristics of surface streams, that is, flowing in a very narrow, ribbon-like pattern. Underground water flows as broad as sheets of water, sometimes miles wide, all seeping in the same direction.

It is suggested that the roots of the stones buried in the ground are subjected to great pressures from these same underground waters. Few writers appear to have read the excavation reports on such stone circles as Stonehenge and Avebury. In few instances have the bases of the stones extend below the water table (the highest level to which underground waters rise) for any significant depth. Hydrostatic pressure increases with depth of water, and it would take depths of many feet to generate any significant amounts of pressure (you can demonstrate this for yourself the next time you are in a swimming pool — dive down to the bottom of the deep end, say about eight feet, and see if you are crushed by the pressure).

With regard to the external forms of crystals, there is definitely a relationship between the shape of a crystal and static electricity, as static electricity tends to accumulate on the points and edges of crystals. Unfortunately for those who attempt to draw conclusions about this, static electricity also accumulates on the points and edges of everything else! Whether it is the point of a pencil, the tip of a cat's tail, the peak of a house or church steeple, or even the corner of a picture frame, in each instance there will be a static electricity accumulation. This is particularly noticeable in drier climates, especially when two people walk across a room with a shag carpet to kiss one another — there is often a bolt of static electricity a quarter of an inch long or more as they get close to one another, and often from distinctly uncomfortable portions of the body!

If this emphasis on outer shape is true, then we might also expect to carve quartz crystals (or at least the shape of quartz crystals) out of blocks of wood, and presume that they would behave exactly as natural crystals. Obviously they do not.

Not only do some authors show a lack of understanding of geology and mineralogy but also of the most basic processes of the lapidary (gem cutter). This lends itself to some rather extraordinary interpretations of certain artefacts from the past, and in particular artefacts with a high degree of emotional impact, such as the crystal skulls which have been found in Latin America.

Such writers tend to view these skulls as isolated artefacts, and do not place them in the context of products of a civilization vastly experienced in stone working and carving. The fact particularly overlooked is that these very same cultures which produced the skulls were producing intricate carvings in jade equally as complex technically and as difficult to execute, as these skulls, and even more complex from the standpoint of the lapidary. Even an amateur lapidary knows that jade is ten times more difficult to shape and carve than quartz crystal.

The writers of these articles, and indeed the 'scientists' who have studied these skulls in laboratories, seem to have the typical layman's misunderstanding of the processes of gem cutting. This viewpoint usually involves an image of a little old man sweating over a stone that he is about to cleave with a blade and a mallet, and then fainting dead away when the stone falls in two perfect pieces! In fact, this particular process is done *very* rarely, and almost always with large diamonds that would take months to saw. Virtually every other type of stone is simply sawn into the desired shape using a diamond impregnated saw blade, and then ground into final shape on horizontal lapping wheels.

It is this misunderstanding that allows the researchers to be 'amazed' that the skulls bear no particular orientation to the crystallographic axes, which would be necessary had they been shaped by cleaving rather than by ordinary grinding methods. Quartz has *no cleavage*, and therefore will not shatter (as the researchers suggest) if the shaping process is not very precise. Truly, the only thing that would have been amazing is if the skulls *had* been oriented to the crystallographic axes.

The researchers also conclude, since there were no particular marks present to suggest it, that no metal tools were used. As a professional lapidary, I would be very interested in seeing what sort of marks one looks for as evidence of metal tools. If a piece is properly executed, there should be no evidence that *any* tools were used. From the lack of these marks, the researchers then conclude that these skulls were probably chiselled into shape using diamonds! Diamonds, although hard, are also quite brittle and shatter easily enough if subjected to sharp blows. Even if metals were not available (and they probably were not) sand drills were. The sand drill is a device commonly used by primitive people even today in various parts of the world for drilling holes in beads and ornaments. In this process a bow drill is used, and the drill 'bit' is often nothing more than a cactus spine which is fed a slurry of fine mud or sand at the point that it enters the rock. As quartz is quite easily ground away by this method, at least compared to jade, one can easily imagine tools of this type scaled up for grinding and shaping larger pieces. With certain types of hard woods and fire-hardened bamboo, metals would be almost unnecessary.

The rough forming of these skulls would have been partly accomplished by sawing or by cobbing, a process of chipping off small pieces until the rough shape is achieved. Cobbing was used to rough shape quartz crystal balls in Japan until well into this century. The tool that may have been used for sawing would be a mud saw, which once again has a modern equivalent. In this tool a single strand of wire (or hemp fibre or fire-hardened bamboo in the ancient tool) is drawn back and forth across the stone, often with a bow for holding the wire taught, and fine mud is fed in along the cut. This process is used today, but with a large metal blade instead of a hempen fibre, for sawing large jade boulders in Alaska.

Some conclude that it would have taken approximately 300 man-years to have made one of these skulls. It would be very surprising if it took two men more than *two* years. There are a great many lapidaries in the world today who could duplicate one of these skulls in approximately that amount of time, using techniques that would have been available 500 or 1000 years ago. Even more amazing than the crystal skulls are the cylinder seals that were produced in Mesopotamia several thousand years before these skulls were made, which are very intricately carved and need a magnifying glass to see all of the detail. Why is it so difficult for us to realize that so-called primitive man knew a thing or two about working stone?

As to the actual uses of these skulls, one need only look again at the culture in which they were produced. Oracular devices, such as 'talking' idols, were not at all uncommon in these cultures, and usually consisted of nothing more than a hole bored through the idol at the location of the mouth. The priest then stood behind the idol (out of sight) and gave the idols 'pronouncements' to the assembled multitudes. As the one crystal skull that has a moving jaw bone also has two small holes on either side of the jaw bone where wires were clearly attached, there is no reason to suspect this skull was anything else. As the human skull was particularly held in respect, and even awe in these early civilizations (as it is even today in ours), then it is easy to imagine the effect of such a 'talking' skull, especially when lit from below, as this skull was apparently designed to be.

There are a great many psychic phenomenon that are described by persons who have been in the presence of these skulls, and this is not surprising. Keep in mind that no matter what its shape, it is still a piece of quartz crystal, and therefore responsive to all of the various energy transformations of such crystals. Because the shape itself is highly emotive even in our 'modern' culture, a person in the presence of such an object will be generating significantly larger amounts of emotional energy.

Another subject worth mentioning is the so called pyramid 'discovered' under the ocean near the Bahamas. There is no need to relate the whole story here, but the one single artefact the diver was able to 'recover' was a 3½-inch quartz crystal ball. It is particularly unfortunate if this ball is to constitute 'proof' of the truth of the story, because quartz balls of that size could be readily purchased through gem suppliers in any major city, and even many amateur lapidaries are making such balls — I have made several myself.

While on the subject of crystal balls, one writer and lecturer has suggested that crystal balls are unsuitable for healing. Assuming that the ball in question is made from a natural material, and not glass, this is a rather extraordinary statement. Remember that the effect of crystals on energy is due to *internal effects*, and has virtually nothing to do with *external* shape. I have recently made a ball of amethyst for a healer, and the reported results have been excellent.

Several 'teachers' around the world are 'manifesting' various gems for their disciples, apparently out of thin air. In the first place, any halfway competent television magician (or more correctly, illusionist) can do the same thing. One such illusionist in Las Vegas was even 'materializing' live tigers on stage. The only difference is that these illusionists are not claiming to be spiritual messiahs.

The second and most telling point concerns the 'gems' themselves. I have had an opportunity to examine some of these, and there are several curious things about them. One 'messiah's' gems are almost all cut into the shape of famous diamonds — but they are not diamond. Such diamond replicas are easily obtained on the commercial market, but they are usually cut from quartz. These indeed appear to be quartz. One of the other 'gems' is a replica of the Hope Diamond, which is blue. This one is cut from *synthetic* sapphire. Are they running out of the real thing on the Other Side?

12.
Workshop Techniques

Through a great deal of recent experience with workshops, several techniques have evolved that demonstrate clearly to the sensitive yet sceptical person that he or she really does have considerable sensitivity to the energies of minerals. Depending on the part of the world in which you live, the subjects of Earth Science, geology, mineralogy, etc., are not often taught to any degree in school, and many workshop participants have virtually no knowledge whatever in these areas. This can actually be an advantage, in that there are no preconceptions to be overcome.

Participants are often asked at the beginning of the workshop whether they feel they have any particular sensitivity to the energies of minerals, and more importantly, whether they do *not*. Usually about half of each group will feel that they have no sensitivity at all to the mineral kingdom. By the end of the first technique described in this section, the so- called 'unsensitive' group will be down to perhaps one, or at the most, two people! Out of groups of twenty people (the average size of the author's workshops) at least nineteen will show definite sensitivities, often to the amazement of the participants.

The workshop techniques described herein can be done by as few as two people, but ideally the group should be larger — at least five or six, and perhaps as many as twenty. The other necessity is, of course, crystals. It is not recommended that personal crystals be used, because the various techniques will require handling of the crystals by other persons in the group; in addition, the user's energies will be imprinted in the crystal, giving an erroneous energy sensation to others who handle it.

As to the way in which the energies are experienced, there seems to be an endless variety, and there is really no 'right' or 'wrong' way. Some people will see images, some will see colours, some will feel the crystals to be heavy or light, some will feel pulsations or perhaps even physical pain, some will experience hot or cold sensations, some will hear sounds and, occasionally, some will even experience odours. Thus, if you are leading a workshop, or just participating in one, it is well to remember, and remind everyone else in the workshop, that the participants should be totally open to whatever experience they have, and to dismiss nothing.

It is also helpful in all of the techniques if there is an opportunity for each person in the group to describe his experiences to the others. What will become immediately apparent is that no matter what the experiment, each person in the group will have experiences different from everyone else. For example, one person may experience a particular crystal as being heavy and hot, whereas the next person may experience the same crystal as being light and airy and quite cool. It follows that the one thing that will also become immediately apparent in using any of these techniques, especially if a group of several or more people are involved, is the inappropriateness of prescribing specific crystals for specific ailments as most 'crystal books' suggest. In one instance you might help the person, but in the other instance, you could very well make things worse. The number of exactly opposite reactions to a particular crystal in a large group is amazing.

As the energies of the planet change with more and more New Age energy, the reactions of crystals will also change, and it is only by constantly re-examining our reactions, and those of others to them, that we can continue to use them properly as spiritual instruments.

Comparison Technique

The objective of the first workshop technique, that of comparison, is not so much to give specific information about the energies of the various crystals used, but to demonstrate clearly to the participant that he or she is indeed sensitive to crystal energies.

The technique begins with the participants sitting in a circle, not in physical contact, with their eyes closed, and one hand open and palm upward to receive a crystal from the leader.

Closing the eyes is important in most workshop techniques in order to limit the amount of information from the ordinary senses that a person receives. Since crystals have no smell or taste (at least in *this* type of experiment!) almost the only sensory input that the participant receives is that of touch; though if the palm of the hand is held open and the crystal is not grasped once it is received from the leader, even this sense is limited. Participants are also instructed to record mentally their very first impression as the crystal comes into the hand, this first impression being the instantaneous intuitive response to the crystal. In this technique, we have eliminated at least 95 per cent of the ordinary sensory inputs to the thinking half of the brain, and therefore the participant is as free as possible to experience his own inner reactions to the crystal.

There is a certain sequence of crystals which has been proven through practice to be particularly useful in comparisons — emphasizing, once again, that the real importance of this technique is to be able to sense the *difference* between the energies of various crystals, and not so much the specific reactions.

The hand in which the crystal is placed is also important, as the energies of the right and left hands vary greatly from one another. It is important in this technique for the left-handed person to reverse the instructions; that is, when a crystal is to be placed into the right hand, the left-handed person should receive it in the left hand instead.

This technique usually begins then by dropping a rock crystal (the colourless variety of quartz) into the right hand of each participant — one crystal per participant. It is also best if no commentary is made by the leader as to which crystal the participants are receiving, in order that as little information as possible be given so as to not conflict with the intuitive mind's response. After all of the crystals have been given out, and the last participants have had perhaps five to ten seconds to sense the energies, the group leader then verbally asks the group to discuss their reactions.

The group should keep their eyes closed until this discussion is finished, as very often colour sensations and sensations of shape and weight will be directly opposite to the crystal that the participant is holding. After everyone has had a chance to share their experience, the group may then open their eyes and see which crystal they have.

The group members are then asked to close their eyes and place the same crystal into their left hand to see if it feels different. Once again, reactions are shared.

Keeping the rock crystal in the left hand, the participants are then asked to close their eyes again and the group leader drops an amethyst crystal into each participant's right hand. Reactions are recorded as before. Then, the group is asked to place the rock crystal on the floor and to transfer the amethyst to the left hand. Once again, eyes are closed, and reactions are shared.

The amethyst is then retained in the left hand for comparison with other types of crystals. In this case, the other crystals may be garnet, topaz, calcite, fluorite, or any other crystals that may be available. If tourmaline and aquamarine crystals are available, they should be kept until last. The tourmaline is used in comparison with the amethyst, and then the amethyst is placed on the floor, and the tourmaline crystal is held in the left hand. If aquamarine crystals are available, then aquamarine is used in comparison with the tourmaline. This comparison can often be quite dramatic.

Sometime after the amethyst has been transferred to the left hand, and the group's eyes are once again closed, a second amethyst crystal should be placed in each participant's right hand. This gives a dramatic comparison of how different crystals of the same mineral can have quite different sensations, once again putting to rest ideas of prescribing specific crystals for specific illnesses.

It is probably apparent that this particular workshop technique can be done with only one person handing the crystals to a second person, but with a larger group it is a great deal more fun, especially when participants begin to have exactly the opposite sensations to those of someone else in the group. If any unpleasant reactions are experienced to any particular crystal, there is no reason to go on holding it. Sometimes such a reaction is a karmic memory of crystal use (or misuse), and the participant may feel drawn to meditate with a crystal that has been unpleasant to discover the source of the reaction.

Interrupted Circle Technique

This technique involves once again sitting in a circle and requires at least four or five people to be effective. Each participant holds a crystal that he or she is comfortable with; in this case personal crystals are acceptable since other members of the group will not handle them. The participants close their eyes, and visualize a flow of energy, beginning either to the left or to the right, around the group. The energy is visualized flowing from one crystal to the next, and in many instances participants will feel a definite tug on their hand in the direction of the energy flow. Then, the leader of the group, holding his own crystal, will replace it with a crystal of another mineral, which should cause either an interruption or some sort of change in the energy flow. Participants should then speak up the instant they perceive a change in the energies, and anyone in the circle who has also felt the change should be invited to describe what he or she has felt. It is interesting to note the amount of time that elapses from the time that a new crystal is put into the circle, until one of the participants senses a change in the energies. In many cases this will be almost instantly. If a participant is particularly sensitive, he may even be able to name the new mineral. It is important of course that there are no visual clues as to which mineral is being substituted or to when the substitution takes place.

Clean/Unclean

In this technique, two crystals of the same mineral (such as amethyst) are used. The leader takes both crystals to a place where he cannot be seen by the group. In one crystal he places a great deal of negative energy through the usual programming techniques; the other crystal is thoroughly cleansed. Both crystals are then taken back to the participants, placed a foot or more apart on the table, and the group is invited to sense which is which.

It is important for the workshop leader to blank his mind during this process in order that no telepathic cues are given to the participants. This can be repeated several times with crystals of different minerals. By all means clean the 'dirty' crystal when you have finished.

Telepathy

Some readers will already be familiar with various types of telepathy experiments, and if you have already done such experiments just add crystals into the techniques that you are already using. For those who have not attempted such techniques, the following is especially recommended.

If you are doing this in a group, or for that matter on a one-to-one basis, it is recommended that a set of symbols are used, which are agreed on beforehand by the group. Five to ten such symbols are sufficient; geometric shapes are particularly useful, as they do not require any interpretation. It is even recommended that the exact shapes being used should be drawn out, either on a set of cards or else on a blackboard, so that everyone will be using the same symbol. A star, for example, may have as few as three points, or as many as you can cram into the space available. So, if a star is to be one of your symbols, agree on a five pointed star, a six pointed star, etc. Other geometric shapes, such as squares, circles, rectangles, and triangles (once again, dimensions vary), should be used. Symbols such as ankhs, crosses, or other symbols which have particular meanings or interpretations should be avoided.

The next stage is for each person in the group to select a crystal, preferably having a number available, with the intent of using it for telepathy. Keep in mind when you choose the crystal that it should be in harmony with other crystals being used for the same experiment at the same time.

One person's crystal can then be used as a 'transmitter' and the others as a 'receiver', remembering that they are not transmitters in the technical sense. This experiment can be done on a one-to-one basis; or the group leader can transmit an image to the entire group, leaving the group to decide which image has been sent. In either case, you may find it necessary to place the crystal in contact with the head: the best place is usually the forehead, in the so-called third-eye position. It is interesting to attempt this sort of experiment both with and without crystals in order to see if the use of crystals will improve the result.

Several persons who have successfully used crystals as telepathic communicators have found it particularly effective to use halves of the same crystal. In this case, of course, it is necessary to have the crystal sawn by a lapidary.

Psychometry

An experiment along similar lines to the telepathy experiment is in programming an image into a crystal and seeing if it can be picked up by another person. In this instance, the image (and once again, it is recommended in the beginning that simple geometric shapes be used) is placed into the crystal using the usual techniques of programming, and the crystal is then handed to another person, or several persons, one at a time: they then attempt to read the image from the crystal by psychometry. The usual technique for psychometry is to place the item — in this case the crystal — over the forehead in the 'third-eye' position, and then attempt to 'see' the image. Again, it is recommended that the images used are selected from a group of images agreed beforehand by the group, although if the group happens to be one that is used to working with telepathic images any image may be used.

Touch for Health

If a member of your group happens to be familiar with the techniques of Touch for Health, then the effect of crystals placed into the aura can be readily demonstrated. It is important in using this method for demonstration that the crystal does not actually touch the body of the person on whom the technique is being demonstrated.

This is different from the usual Touch for Health technique of either massaging or putting pressure directly onto the particular energy point. In this case, the speed of the results will vary from crystal to crystal.

It is apparent from the techniques described above that a small amount of experimentation can provide a great deal of information about crystals, but that it can also be a great deal of fun! There are plenty of experiments you can devise for yourself. Let your imagination be your guide.

13.

Growing Your Own Crystals

It is quite simple to grow crystals yourself. These are crystals that grow naturally and are perfectly happy to do so under the conditions which exist in your own home. The crystals are all grown from water solutions and will form easily at room temperature. The process is not unlike the processes described in Chapter 4, except in those instances the solution was of molten rock.

The equipment that you will need for this can easily be found around the home, and consists of a saucepan of about a quart (one litre) capacity, a shallow glass dish such as a glass pie dish, and a quart (one litre) capacity fruit jar. All of the containers must be thoroughly washed and carefully dried so that no oil, grease or other foreign material is present.

Since the crystals are grown in a water solution, it is desirable to have the water as pure as possible. Distilled water is often available, which can be purchased in large grocery stores for use in steam irons, or even bottled spring water (non-carbonated) with a low mineral content is acceptable. If neither of these are available ordinary tap water will do, but often chemicals and minerals in tap water will affect crystallization slightly.

There are several chemicals which will grow lovely crystals; these are listed at the end of this chapter. There are several listed that are poisonous and these should not be used in areas where food is either handled or prepared; all containers used for these chemicals should be carefully washed two or three times after each usage. Also, of course, keep all of this out of reach of children, who are usually quite fascinated by the whole process and who often have a tendency to put pretty things into their mouth. Don't let this discourage you, though, as most of the chemicals are quite harmless and will produce magnificent results.

The solution which we will prepare first is called a saturated solution, meaning that the water has dissolved as much of the solid chemical as it can hold. Therefore as the water evaporates, some of the dissolved chemical must be released, and this is what forms crystals.

The first part of the process is to fill the saucepan with water and heat it until it is just warm. It is not necessary to boil it: heat it to just above room temperature. Having warmed the water, begin to stir in amounts of whatever chemical you have chosen for crystal growth. It will be necessary to stir the water constantly, to be certain that all the solid chemicals are dissolving, and you should keep adding solids as long as they will dissolve. When you have reached the point where no more will dissolve, and there is a solid residue in the bottom of the pan, you are finished with *Stage I*.

For *Stage II*, allow the pan to sit without any further heat for ten to fifteen minutes. This will ensure that the last possible solids are going to dissolve; any leftover solids will settle to the bottom of the pan.

For *Stage III*, pour about half an inch to an inch (2.2cm) of solution from the pan into the shallow glass dish. Set the glass dish aside in a dust-free place, and also in a place where the family pets are unlikely to drink from it. Then, take the remainder of the solution from the pan, pour it gently into the fruit jar, and cover tightly.

In a few days, crystals will begin to appear in the bottom of the glass dish and you should allow them to continue to form until they are approximately a quarter of an inch across (5mm), or until they begin to grow into one another. When they have reached the appropriate size, we are ready to go on to the next stage (Figure 128).

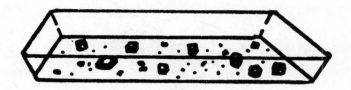

Figure 128   Seed crystals forming in glass dish

For *Stage IV*, we need our saucepan once again. Carefully tip the liquid remaining in the glass dish down the sink, if possible without disturbing the crystals on the bottom. Now, using cold water from the tap, gently run about another half inch of water into the glass dish, and gently pour it out again almost at once. Once again the used water can just go down the drain, as we have only used it to rinse the crystals in the bottom of the dish. Allow the crystals to air-dry: it is extremely important at this stage to keep them as clean as possible and not to handle them (it will be a temptation). One of these crystals will then form the seed crystal for the larger crystal that you will grow in the fruit jar.

After the crystals have dried, wash your hands thoroughly to remove as much natural oil as possible; then sort through the crystals in the bottom of the dish to find the largest and most perfect. If possible, try to find one that has no other crystals growing from it. Then, take your chosen seed crystal and using a piece of white thread (cotton) carefully loop it once around the seed crystal and tie a knot. You may have to make several attempts at this; should it prove impossible to do, then choose another seed crystal that is perhaps a slightly better shape.

We now return to the fruit jar of solution, which was set aside several days ago. Even though the jar has been sealed, there will probably be small crystals forming on the bottom, as the result of the cooling down of the solution. Carefully empty the contents of the jar back into the clean saucepan, being careful not to disturb the crystals on the bottom of the jar. If we were to leave these crystals on the bottom, they would provide other crystallizing surfaces for

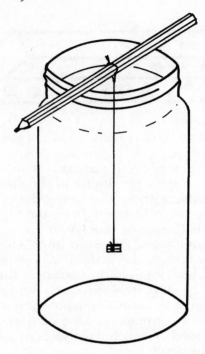

Figure 129   Seed crystal suspended in jar

the remainder of the solution, which would considerably slow down the growth of the seed crystal. Having emptied the jar of its liquid contents, take the jar to the sink, empty out the small crystals from the bottom and wash the jar thoroughly in clean water. This will assure us of an absolutely fresh start. Now, return the contents of the saucepan to the jar, and measure off the appropriate length of thread (cotton) so that the seed crystal is supported about two inches (4.5cm) from the bottom of the jar. Tie the thread (cotton) around a pencil and place the pencil across the opening of the fruit jar so that the seed crystal is suspended in the remaining liquid (Figure 129).

In the last stage, cover the top of the jar with gauze, or some other material that will allow the water in the jar to evaporate but will keep dust and other debris out of the jar. The ideal location for the jar is somewhere with an even temperature, such as an airing cupboard; or, if you have central heating, a room where the temperature is maintained. Any major changes in temperature, will cause irregular crystal growth. Since the objective is to allow the water in the jar to evaporate, thereby making solid chemicals available for crystal growth, the jar should be kept in a warm room rather than a cold one.

You will begin to see results within a few days, and although it may take a month or more to grow a crystal an inch across, you will be surprised at the day-to-day progress. You will obviously wish to watch the growth of your crystal, but try to place the jar in a location where you will not have to move it in order to observe the growth. The less the jar is disturbed during the growing process, the better. Also, the more constant the growing conditions, the more perfect the final crystal will be. You will notice that the larger the crystal gets, the less perfect it will become. Now you can begin to appreciate the processes that take place in nature to form large, perfect crystals!

If you wish to try to grow crystals larger than about an inch in size, it may be necessary to prepare a second batch of solution and replace the original batch, which will now be much depleted in volume. Should you decide to do this, do not handle the crystal between changes of solution, as any oil from your fingers on the crystal will cause major irregularities in its growth. All that is necessary is simply to lift the crystal out of the jar using the pencil, hang it somewhere safely, such as inside another empty jar, and then empty the old solution from the growing jar, and wash it clean. Prepare a new solution as in Stage I and place the new solution in the growing jar, having allowed it to cool to room temperature first. Replace the crystal and allow it to continue growing. Remember that the larger the crystal gets, the slower the growth will be, since larger numbers of atoms are required for larger faces.

When the crystal has grown to the size required, remove it from the solution, wash it for a few seconds in cold water (if you use hot water it will partially dissolve the crystal), and pat it dry with a paper towel. Finally snip the remaining thread (cotton) from the crystal. Keep in mind that your crystal is soluble in water and should be kept in a dry place; also that the crystals grown by this method can be scratched quite readily and will be somewhat brittle. They are certainly strong enough for ordinary handling, but they will not stand up to being dropped on hard surfaces.

If you wish to grow several crystals at one time, just make a larger batch of solution and use several jars at once, each with a different seed crystal. It is recommended that only one crystal be grown per jar; when several are grown in the same jar, growth is very slow and the crystals will often be less perfect.

If you wish to programme the crystal through its growth stages, then use one of the methods described in Chapter 8. Should you decide to use other crystals to help programme the ones that you are growing, then the 'assisting' crystals can be placed in the same jar. Unless the 'assisting' crystal is water-soluble, and most of them will not be, there is no harm in placing it in the growing solution. Just be certain that it is washed clean before it is put in, as any oil or dust in the growing solution can cause irregularities in the crystal that you are attemting to grow.

Depending on the country in which you live, the following chemical names may differ somewhat. Consult with your local druggist or chemist, who will probably know the local name.

1.   Alum (Potassium Alum) — this is highly recommended as it grows beautiful octahedral crystals with relative ease. It is non-poisonous, and is used in making pickles.
2.   Rochelle Salt — grows oblong colourless crystals, which often take some quite startling prismatic shapes. (Non-poisonous.)
3.   Sugar — these are quite easy to grow, but instead of forming a single crystal sugar will often try to form a chain of crystals growing up the thread.
4.   Copper Sulphate (Blue Vitriol) — this is *highly poisonous* if taken internally, but if you are careful, this will produce brilliant blue crystals.
5.   Potassium Ferrocyanide — *poisonous* if taken internally. Produces beautiful lemon yellow crystals.

6.   Potassium Ferriayanide — *poisonous* if taken internally. Produces ruby-red crystals. If you wish to colour the sugar or alum crystals, a drop of coloured ink or food colouring in the solution will have the desired effect.

Many readers will object to growing crystals on the grounds that they are not generated in a natural environment: but such crystals are not meant to replace natural crystals, and one hopes that they will be grown to increase the crystal user's appreciation of natural processes.

Even if only one or two are grown, it is important for the grower to programme in as much natural energy into the growing crystal as possible, beginning with the seed. If the final crystals still don't 'feel' right, they can always be re-dissolved and poured down the drain.

Meditating with these crystals as they form can be very rewarding as you will have an opportunity to become involved with the elemental of the crystal as it fulfills its own Act of Creation, and such an insight can give you a further insight into the nature of matter itself, helping to further your own insight into yourself – also a synthesis of matter and spirit. A cousin of crystals.

Further Information
Ra Bonewitz
182 Southfield Road
London W4.
ENGLAND
(SAE appreciated)

Index